P9-CLX-928

HOW TO
MAKE YOUR
OWN WILL

with forms

2nd Edition

Mark Warda
Attorney at Law

SPHINX® PUBLISHING
A Division of Sourcebooks, Inc.®
Naperville, IL

ALEXANDRIA LIBRARY
ALEXANDRIA, VA 22314

Copyright © 1988, 1993, 1995, 1998, 2000 by Mark Warda
Cover design © 2000 by Sourcebooks, Inc.®

All rights reserved. No part of this book may be reproduced in any form or by any electronic or mechanical means including information storage and retrieval systems—except in the case of brief quotations embodied in critical articles or reviews—without permission in writing from its publisher, Sourcebooks, Inc. Purchasers of the book are granted license to use the forms contained herein for their own personal use. No claim of copyright is made to any government form reproduced herein. The living will contained in this book is from the book *How to Write Your Own Living Will*, ©1998 Edward A. Haman and is used with permission.

Second Edition, 2000
Information Reviewed, 1/2001
Published by: **Sphinx® Publishing, a division of Sourcebooks, Inc.®**

<u>Naperville Office</u>
P.O. Box 4410
Naperville, Illinois 60567-4410
630-961-3900
Fax: 630-961-2168

Cover and Interior Design: Sourcebooks, Inc.®

This publication is designed to provide accurate and authoritative information in regard to the subject matter covered. It is sold with the understanding that the publisher is not engaged in rendering legal, accounting, or other professional service. If legal advice or other expert assistance is required, the services of a competent professional person should be sought.

From a Declaration of Principles Jointly Adopted by a Committee of the
American Bar Association and a Committee of Publishers and Associations

This product is not a substitute for legal advice.

Disclaimer required by Texas statutes.

Library of Congress Cataloging-in-Publication Data
Warda, Mark.
    How to make your own will : with forms / Mark Warda.--2nd. ed.
      p.   cm.
    Includes index.
    ISBN 1-57248-119-6 (pbk.)
    1. Wills--United States--Popular works. I. Title

KF755.Z9 W35 2000
346.7305'4--dc21

                    00-030745
                    CIP

Printed and bound in the United States of America.

VHG Paperback — 10 9 8 7 6 5 4 3 2

CONTENTS

Using Self-Help Law Books

Before using a self-help law book, you should realize the advantages and disadvantages of doing your own legal work and understand the challenges and diligence that this requires.

THE GROWING
TREND
Rest assured that you won't be the first or only person handling your own legal matter. For example, in some states, more than seventy-five percent of the people in divorces and other cases represent themselves. Because of the high cost of legal services, this is a major trend and many courts are struggling to make it easier for people to represent themselves. However, some government offices are not happy with people who do not use attorneys and refuse to help them in any way. For some, the attitude is, "Go to the law library and figure it out for yourself."

We write and publish self-help law books to give people an alternative to the often complicated and confusing legal books found in most law libraries. We have made the explanations of the law as simple and easy to understand as possible. Of course, unlike an attorney advising an individual client, we cannot cover every conceivable possibility.

COST/VALUE
ANALYSIS
Whenever you shop for a product or service, you are faced with various levels of quality and price. In deciding what product or service to buy, you make a cost/value analysis on the basis of your willingness to pay and the quality you desire.

When buying a car, you decide whether you want transportation, comfort, status, or sex appeal. Accordingly, you decide among such choices as a Neon, a Lincoln, a Rolls Royce, or a Porsche. Before making a decision, you usually weigh the merits of each option against the cost.

When you get a headache, you can take a pain reliever (such as aspirin) or visit a medical specialist for a neurological examination. Given this choice, most people, of course, take a pain reliever, since it costs only pennies; whereas a medical examination costs hundreds of dollars and takes a lot of time. This is usually a logical choice because it is rare to need anything more than a pain reliever for a headache. But in some cases, a headache may indicate a brain tumor and failing to see a specialist right away can result in complications. Should everyone with a headache go to a specialist? Of course not, but people treating their own illnesses must realize that they are betting on the basis of their cost/value analysis of the situation. They are taking the most logical option.

The same cost/value analysis must be made when deciding to do one's own legal work. Many legal situations are very straight forward, requiring a simple form and no complicated analysis. Anyone with a little intelligence and a book of instructions can handle the matter without outside help.

But there is always the chance that complications are involved that only an attorney would notice. To simplify the law into a book like this, several legal cases must often be condensed into a single sentence or paragraph. Otherwise, the book would be several hundred pages long and too complicated for most people. However, this simplification necessarily leaves out many details and nuances that would apply to special or unusual situations. Also, there are many ways to interpret most legal questions.

Therefore, in deciding to use a self-help law book and to do your own legal work, you must realize that you are making a cost/value analysis. You have decided that the money you will save in doing it yourself outweighs the chance that your case will not turn out to your satisfaction. Most people handling their own simple legal matters never have a problem, but occasionally people find that it ended up costing them more to have an attorney straighten out the situation than it would have if they had hired an attorney in the beginning. Keep this in mind while handling your case, and be sure to consult an attorney if you feel you might need further guidance.

LOCAL RULES   The next thing to remember is that a book which covers the law for the entire nation, or even for an entire state, cannot possibly include every procedural difference of every jurisdiction. Whenever possible, we provide the exact form needed; however, in some areas, each county may require unique forms and procedures. In our state books, our forms usually cover the majority of counties in the state, or provide examples of the type of form which will be required. In our national books, our forms are sometimes even more general in nature but are designed to give a good idea of the type of form that will be needed in most locations. Nonetheless, keep in mind that your state or county may have a requirement, or use a form, that is not included in this book.

You should not necessarily expect to be able to get all of the information and resources you need solely from within the pages of this book. This book will serve as your guide, giving you specific information whenever possible and helping you to find out what else you will need to know. This is just like if you decided to build your own backyard deck. You might purchase a book on how to build decks. However, such a book would not include the building codes and permit requirements of every city, town, county, and township in the nation; nor would it include the lumber, nails, saws, hammers, and other materials and tools you would need to actually build the deck. You would use the book as your guide, and then do some work and research involving such matters as whether you need a permit of some kind, what type and grade of wood are available in your area, whether to use hand tools or power tools, and how to use those tools.

Before using the forms in a book like this, you should check with your secretary of state or local government office to see if there are any local rules of which you should be aware, or local forms you will need to use. Often, such forms will require the same information as the forms in the book but are merely laid out differently or use slightly different language. They will sometimes require additional information.

CHANGES IN THE LAW

Besides being subject to local rules and practices, the law is subject to change at any time. The courts and the legislatures of all fifty states are constantly revising the laws. It is possible that while you are reading this book, some aspect of the law is being changed.

In most cases, the change will be of minimal significance. A form will be redesigned, additional information will be required, or a waiting period will be extended. As a result, you might need to revise a form, file an extra form, or wait out a longer time period; these types of changes will not usually affect the outcome of your case. On the other hand, sometimes a major part of the law is changed, the entire law in a particular area is rewritten, or a case that was the basis of a central legal point is overruled. In such instances, your entire ability to pursue your case may be impaired.

To help you with local requirements and changes in the law, be sure to read the section in chapter 1 on "Finding the Law: Legal Research."

Again, you should weigh the value of your case against the cost of an attorney and make a decision as to what you believe is in your best interest.

INTRODUCTION

This book was written to help you quickly and easily make your own will without the expense or delay of hiring a lawyer. It begins with a short explanation of how a will works and what a will can and cannot do. It is designed to allow those with simple estates to quickly and inexpensively set up their affairs to distribute their property according to their wishes. It includes an explanation of how such things as joint property and "pay on death" accounts affect your planning.

It also includes information on appointing a guardian for any minor children you may have. This can be useful in avoiding bad feelings between relatives and in protecting the children from being raised by someone to whom you would object.

Chapters 1 through 5 explain the laws that affect the making of a will Chapters 6 and 7 explain living wills and organ donor cards. After chapter 7 is a glossary which you should use if there are any words in the text which you do not understand. Appendix A contains tables of some of the laws referred to in the text as to each state. Appendix B contains sample filled-in will forms to show you how it is done. Appendix C contains blank will forms you can use.

You can prepare your own will quickly and easily by using the forms out of the book, or by photocopying them, or you can retype the material on sheets of paper. The small amount of time it takes to do this can give you and your loved ones the peace of mind of knowing that your estate will be distributed according to your wishes.

A surprising number of people have had their estates pass to the wrong parties because of a simple lack of knowledge of how the laws work. Before using any of the forms in appendix C, you should read and understand all of the previous chapters of this book.

In each example given in the text you might ask, "What if the spouse died first?" or "What if the children were grown up?" and then the answer might be different. If your situation is at all complicated, you are advised to seek the advice of an attorney. In many communities, wills are available for very reasonable prices. No book of this type can cover every contingency in every case, but a knowledge of the basics will help you to make the right decisions regarding your property.

The forms in this book are for simple wills to leave property to your family, or if you have no family, to friends or charities. As explained in chapter 2, if you wish to disinherit your family and leave your property to others, you should consult with an attorney who can make sure that your will cannot be successfully challenged in court.

There is no worse torture than the torture of laws.
—Francis Bacon

BASIC RULES YOU SHOULD KNOW

1

Before making your will, you should understand how a will works and what it can and cannot do. Otherwise, your plans may not be carried out and the wrong people may end up with your property.

WHAT IS A WILL?

A will is a document you can use to control who gets your property, who will be guardian of your children and their property, and who will manage your estate upon your death.

HOW A WILL IS USED

Some people think a will avoids probate. It does not. A will is the document used in probate to determine who receives the property, and who is appointed guardian and executor or personal representative.

AVOIDING PROBATE

If you wish to avoid probate, you need to use methods other than a will, such as joint ownership, pay-on-death accounts, or living trusts. The first two of these are discussed later in this chapter. For information on living trusts, you should refer to a book which focuses on trusts as used for estate planning. *Living Trusts and Simple Ways to Avoid Probate* is available from the publisher of this book.

If a person successfully avoids probate with all of his or her property, then he or she may not need a will. In most cases, when a husband or wife dies no will or probate is necessary because everything is owned jointly. However, everyone should have a will in case some property does not avoid probate (For example, if one forgot to put it into joint ownership or it was received just prior to death, or if both husband and wife die in the same accident.)

JOINT TENANCY AVOIDS PROBATE

Property that is owned in *joint tenancy with right of survivorship* does not pass under a will. If a will gives property to one person but it is already in a joint account with another person, the will is usually ignored and the joint owner of the account gets the property. This is because the property in the account avoids probate and passes directly to the joint owner. A will only controls property that goes through probate. There are exceptions to this rule. If money is put into a joint account only for convenience, it might pass under the will; but if the joint owner does not give it up, it could take an expensive court battle to get it back.

Putting property into joint tenancy does not give absolute rights to it. If the estate owes estate taxes, the recipient of joint tenancy property may have to contribute to the tax payment. Also, some states give spouses a right to property that is in joint accounts with other people. This is explained later in this chapter.

EXAMPLES ☞ Ted and his wife want all of their property to go to the survivor of them. They put their house, cars, bank accounts, and brokerage accounts in joint ownership. When Ted dies his wife only has to show his death certificate to get all the property transferred to her name. No probate or will is necessary.

☞ After Ted's death, his wife, Michelle puts all of the property and accounts into joint ownership with her son, Mark. Upon her death, Mark needs only to present her death certificate to have everything transferred into his name. No probate or will is necessary.

JOINT TENANCY OVERRULES YOUR WILL

If all property is in joint ownership or if all property is distributed through a will, things are simple. But when some property passes by each method, a person's plans may not be fulfilled.

EXAMPLES

☞ Bill's will leaves all his property to his sister, Mary. Bill dies owning a house jointly with his wife, Joan, and a bank account jointly with his son, Don. Upon Bill's death Joan gets the house, Don gets the bank account and his sister, Mary, gets nothing.

☞ Betty's will leaves half her assets to Ann and half her assets to George. Betty dies owning $1,000,000 in stock jointly with George, and a car in her name alone. Ann gets only a half interest in the car. George gets all the stock and a half interest in the car.

☞ John's will leaves all his property equally to his five children. Before going in the hospital he puts his oldest son, Harry, as a joint owner of his accounts. John dies and Harry gets all of his assets. The rest of the children get nothing.

In each of these cases, the property went to a person it probably shouldn't have because the decedent didn't realize that joint ownership overruled his or her will. This might not be a problem in some families. Harry might divide the property equally (and possibly pay a gift tax). But in many cases, Harry would just keep everything and the family would never talk to him again, or would take him to court.

JOINT TENANCY CAN BE RISKY

In many cases joint property can be an ideal way to own property and avoid probate. However it does have risks. If you put your real estate in joint ownership with someone, you cannot sell it or mortgage it without that person's signature. If you put your bank account in joint ownership with someone they can take out all of your money.

EXAMPLES

☞ Alice put her house in joint ownership with her son. She later married Ed and moved in with him. She wanted to sell her house and to invest the money for income. Her son refused to sign the deed because he wanted to keep the home in the family. She was in court for ten months getting her house back and the judge almost refused to do it.

☞ Alex put his bank accounts into joint ownership with his daughter Mary to avoid probate. Mary fell in love with Doug who was in trouble with the law. Doug talked Mary into "borrowing" $30,000 from the account for a "business deal" that went sour. Later she "borrowed" $25,000 more to pay Doug's bail bond. Alex didn't find out until it was too late that his money was gone.

"TENANCY IN COMMON" DOES NOT AVOID PROBATE

In most states, there are three basic ways to own property, joint tenancy with right of survivorship, tenancy in common, and an estate by the entireties. *Joint tenancy with right of survivorship* means that if one owner of the property dies, the survivor automatically gets the decedent's share. *Tenancy in common* means when one owner dies, that owner's share of the property goes to his or her heirs or beneficiaries under the will. *An estate by the entireties* is like joint tenancy with right of survivorship, but it can only apply to a married couple and is only recognized in some states.

EXAMPLES

☞ Tom and Marcia bought a house together and lived together for twenty years but were never married. The deed did not specify joint tenancy. When Tom died, his bother inherited his half of the house and it had to be sold because Marcia could not afford to buy it from him.

☞ Lindsay and her husband Rocky bought a house. When Rocky suddenly died, Lindsay obtained full ownership of the house by filing a death certificate at the courthouse. That was because the deed to the house stated that they were husband and wife so ownership was presumed to be tenancy by the entireties.

A Spouse Can Overrule a Will

Under the laws of most states, a surviving spouse is entitled to a percentage of a person's estate no matter what the person's will states. This percentage can range from one-quarter to one-half and is usually called an *elective share* or a *forced share*. In some states, the share is only calculated on the assets passing through probate; but in other states, the share includes property that avoids probate. In some states, the share depends on whether the property is *marital property* or *separate property*. This is determined by whether the property was acquired before or during the marriage, whether it was mixed with marital property, and whether it came from some source outside the marriage.

EXAMPLES

☞ John owns a $1,000,000 ranch with his brother in joint tenancy with right of survivorship and $1,000,000 in stock in his own name. His will leaves his stock to his children by a prior marriage, and nothing to his wife because she is wealthier than him and does not need the money. In some states, unless John has a premarital or marital agreement with his wife, she would be entitled to claim one-third of the stock.

In other states, his wife could claim one-half of the stock and one-half of the ranch.

In some states, a spouse can claim a portion of the estate only for the term of his or her life.

☞ Mary puts half of her property in a joint account with her husband and in her will she leaves all of her other property to her sister. When she dies, her husband gets all the money in the joint account and thirty percent of all her other property.

If you do not plan to leave your spouse at least the amount of property your state allows by statute, you should consult a lawyer. Appendix A contains a state-by-state list of the spouse's share as of the time of completion of this manuscript. (Laws are amended regularly, so you should check your state law to see if it has been amended.)

A SPOUSE'S SHARE CAN BE AVOIDED

While some feel it is wrong to avoid giving a spouse the share allowed by law, there are legitimate reasons for doing so (such as where there are children from a prior marriage) and the law allows exceptions.

The safest way is for both spouses to sign a written agreement either before or after the marriage waiving any share the law may give them in each others' estates. However, while many spouses express the greatest fondness for their stepchildren, getting them to sign over a large share of his or her estate can be a challenge.

In some states a spouse's share can be avoided partially or completely by owning property in joint tenancy or in a trust. It is necessary in some cases, but not in all, to have the spouse sign over any interest he or she may have.

EXAMPLE   ☞ Dan owns his stocks jointly with his son. He owns his bank accounts jointly with his daughter. If he has no other property, in many states his spouse gets nothing since there is no property in his estate.

This is what would happen in a state where the spouse is entitled to a share of the *probate estate*. However, in some states, the spouse would be entitled to a share of the *augmented estate*. This is all assets which passed upon the death of the owner (such as joint property, life insurance and beneficial interests in trusts. See appendix A for your state's laws. However, keep in mind that these laws can change at any time, so if this is a concern to you check with an estate planning attorney.

Another way to leave something to someone other than your spouse and avoid the forced share is with a life insurance policy naming someone other than your spouse as beneficiary. However, in some states, this can also be included in the estate.

Avoiding a spouse's share, especially without his or her knowledge, opens the possibility of a lawsuit after your death, and if your actions were not done to precise legal requirements, they could be overruled by a court. Therefore, you should consider consulting an attorney if you plan to leave your spouse less than the share provided by law.

I/T/F Bank Accounts Are Better Than Joint Ownership

One way of keeping bank accounts out of your estate and still retain control is to title them *in trust for* or I/T/F with a named a beneficiary. Some banks may use the letters POD for *pay on death* or TOD for *transfer on death*. Either way the result is the same. No one except you can get the money until your death, and on death it immediately goes directly to the person you name, without a will or probate proceeding. These are sometimes called *Totten Trusts* after the court case that declared them legal.

EXAMPLE

☛ Rich opened a bank account in the name of "Rich, I/T/F Mary." If Rich dies, the money automatically goes to Mary, but prior to his death Mary has no control over the account, doesn't even have to know about it, and Rich can take Mary's name off the account at any time.

SECURITIES CAN BE REGISTERED I/T/F IN SOME STATES

The drawback of the Totten Trust has been that it is only good for cash in a bank account. Stocks and bonds still had to go through probate. But beginning in 1990, states began enacting a new law allowing I/T/F accounts for securities. These can include stocks, bonds, mutual funds, and other similar investments. Now an estate with cash and securities can pass on death with no need for court proceedings.

At the time of publication of this book, the law has been passed by forty-two states, and the other eight may pass it soon. Check with your mutual fund, stock broker, attorney, or in your state statutes. The law is called the Uniform TOD Securities Registration Act. The states that have passed this law are listed in appendix A.

To set up your securities to transfer automatically on death, you need to have them correctly registered. If you use a brokerage account, the brokerage company should have a form for you to do this.

If your state has not passed this law, you may be able to still get the benefits of it by moving your securities account to a firm in a state which has passed this law. Check with different stock brokers and mutual fund companies to see if they allow you to set up your account to transfer on death.

If your securities are registered in your own name or with your spouse, you need to reregister them in TOD format with the designation of your beneficiary. The following are examples of how it is done in many states. Check with your mutual fund or stock broker for the proper way in your state or get a copy of the statute cited in the appendix.

Sole owner with sole beneficiary:

```
John S. Brown TOD John S. Brown Jr.
```

Multiple owners with sole beneficiary (John and Mary are joint tenants with right of survivorship and when they die, John, Jr., inherits the property):

```
John S. Brown Mary B. Brown JT TEN TOD John
S. Brown Jr.
```

Multiple owners-substituted beneficiary (John and Mary are joint tenants with right of survivorship and when they die John Jr. inherits the property, but if John predeceases them, then Peter inherits it):

```
John S. Brown Mary B. Brown JT TEN TOD John
S. Brown Jr. SUB BEN Peter Q. Brown
```

Multiple owners-lineal descendants (John and Mary are joint tenants with right of survivorship and when they die John, Jr., inherits the property, but if John predeceases them then John, Jr.'s lineal descendants inherit it):

```
John S. Brown Mary B. Brown JT TEN TOD John
S. Brown Jr. LDPS
```

THERE ARE SPECIAL RULES FOR HOMESTEADS

In some states, there are special rules for who can inherit your homestead. If you have a spouse, minor children, or both, you may not be able to leave the home to anyone but them.

Homestead laws have some benefits since in some states they cannot be claimed by creditors of the estate.

If you have a spouse or minor children, and plan to leave your homestead to anyone but them, you should see a lawyer.

Some Property May Be Exempt from Your Will

If you have a spouse or minor children, then a certain amount of household furniture, furnishings, and appliances in your "usual place of abode," and perhaps automobiles in your name that are regularly used by you or members of your family are exempt from your will. This is called *exempt property*. If you have a spouse, your spouse gets this property and if you have no spouse, your children get it. Additionally, a spouse or minor children may get a *family allowance*.

EXAMPLE

☞ Donna dies with a will giving half her property to her husband and half to her grown son from a previous marriage. Donna's property consists of a $5,000 automobile, $5,000 in furniture and $10,000 in cash. Donna's husband may be able to get the car and the furniture as exempt property and $6,000 as a family allowance. Then he and the son would split the remaining $4,000. (The son would get even less if the husband also claimed a *spouse's share* as described on page 11.)

In some states, one can avoid having property declared exempt by specifically giving it to someone in a will. If certain items are specifically given to certain persons, those items will not be considered part of the exempt property. In some states, cash kept in a joint or I/T/F bank account would go to the joint owner or beneficiary and not be used as the family allowance. If this may be an issue in your estate, you should check with a lawyer.

Getting Married May Automatically Change Your Will

In some states, if you get married after making your will and do not rewrite it after the wedding, your spouse gets a share of your estate as if you had no will unless you have a pre-marital agreement, or you made a provision for your spouse in the will, or you stated specifically in the will that you intended not to mention your prospective spouse.

EXAMPLE   ☛ John made his will leaving everything to his brother. When he married Joan, an heiress with plenty of money, he didn't change his will because he still wanted his brother to get his estate. When he died, Joan got his entire estate and his brother got nothing.

However, in some states getting married does not change your will. Therefore, if you forget to make a new one, your new spouse may be omitted. See the rule for your state in appendix A.

GETTING DIVORCED MAY AUTOMATICALLY CHANGE YOUR WILL

In some states, getting divorced automatically deletes your former spouse's share from your will. However, you should not rely on this, and you should make a new will. If your spouse tries to get a share of the estate because he or she is mentioned, it may cost your estate considerable legal fees to defeat the claim.

EXAMPLE   ☛ George and Eunice made their wills leaving half their property to each other and half to their children from their previous marriages. After their divorce, George forgot to make a new will. When George died, Eunice hired a lawyer to file papers claiming half the estate. His children's lawyer pointed out that her share was void because of the divorce, but the other lawyer demanded a trial, hoping the children would settle the case by giving his client a few thousand dollars. They refused to settle but their attorney charged $5,000 for the trial.

In some states, divorce does *not* revoke your will. If you do not have time to make a new will after your divorce, you may want to revoke your will. This can be done by tearing it up or by other ways discussed in chapter 5. By revoking your will, you are choosing to use your state's distribution system of deciding your heirs, which, in all cases, would not include your ex-spouse. See chapter 2.

HAVING CHILDREN MAY AUTOMATICALLY CHANGE YOUR WILL

In most states, having a child would change your will to the effect that the new child would get a share equal to that of the other children. However, in some states, having a child may revoke your will or result in the new child getting a larger share than the other children.

EXAMPLE ☞ Dave made a will leaving half his estate to his sister and the other half to his three children. He later had another child and didn't revise his will. In some states, upon his death, his fourth child would get one quarter of his estate, his sister would get three-eighths and the other three children would each get one-eighth.

It is best to rewrite your will at the birth of a child. However, another solution is to include the following clause after the names of your children in your will.

> "...and any afterborn children living at the time of my death, in equal shares."

HOW YOUR DEBTS ARE PAID

One of the duties of the person administering an estate is to pay the debts of the decedent. Before an estate is distributed, the legitimate debts must be ascertained and paid.

An exception is *secured debts*, these are debts that are protected by a lien against property, like a home loan or a car loan. In the case of a secured debt, the loan does not have to be paid before the property is distributed.

EXAMPLE ☞ John owns a $100,000 house with a $80,000 mortgage and he has $100,000 in the bank. If he leaves the house to his brother and the bank account to his sister, his brother would get the home but would owe the $80,000 mortgage.

What if your debts are more than your property? Today, unlike hundreds of years ago, people cannot inherit other peoples' debts. A person's property is used to pay their probate and funeral expenses first, and if there is not enough left to pay their other debts, then the creditors are out of luck. However, if a person leaves property to people and does not have enough assets to pay his or her debts, the property will be sold to pay the debts.

EXAMPLE ☞ Jeb's will leaves all of his property to his three children. At the time of his death, Jeb, has $30,000 in medical bills, $11,000 in credit card debt, and his only assets are his car and $5,000 in stock. The car and stock would be sold and the funeral bill and probate fees paid out of the proceeds. If any money was left, it would go to the creditors and nothing would be left for the children. The children would not have to pay the balances on the medical bills or credit card debt.

In many states, the creditors of a deceased person can only make claims against property which goes through probate. This means that if a person sets up his property so that it all avoids probate, any debts remaining at his death will not have to be paid.

EXAMPLE ☞ When Chris died, he owned a $100,000 house with his wife, a $25,000 bank account with his wife, a ranch worth $200,000 owned jointly with his brother and $20,000 in stock in trust for his children. His debts were $5,000 on a personal credit card and a $20,000 business in his name alone. Because all of his property will pass to people without a probate, in many states, his debts will not have to be paid and the heirs will get the property free and clear.

ESTATE AND INHERITANCE TAXES

Estate taxes are those which are levied against the amount in the estate and inheritance taxes are those which are levied against what is received by a person as an inheritance from an estate.

FEDERAL TAXES The federal government only taxes estates which are greater than $675,000. This amount will rise over the next few years according to the following schedule so that by 2006 only estates over $1 million will be taxed.

Year	Amount
2000-2001	$675,000
2002-2003	$700,000
2004	$850,000
2005	$950,000
2006	$1,000,000

The amounts in the above table are called the *unified credit*. This is the amount of the estate exempt from tax. The unified credit applies to the estate a person leaves at death as well as to gifts during the lifetime. This means that if you make a gift of, say, $50,000 during your life, then the unified credit on your estate will be $50,000 lower than the above amounts.

EXAMPLE ☞ Just before his death in 2002, Phillip gave $500,000 to his sister. When his estate was probated, only the first $200,000 is exempt from tax and the rest is subject to federal estate taxes.

However, there is also an *annual exclusion* of $10,000 per person. This means that every year you can give any person $10,000 and it won't count toward the unified credit. A married couple can make double this amount, or $20,000. The amount will be indexed for inflation but only in $1,000 increments once the total inflation reaches that amount.

Since this amount has not changed in many years there are some congressmen who are trying to pass a law to double the annual exclusion.

EXAMPLE

☞ Edna would like to give her five children each $50,000. She gives them each $10,000 per year for five years so that it doesn't take away from her unified credit.

STATE TAXES

There is a big difference among the states as to whether and how much estates are taxed. Most states do not tax estates unless the estates are very large, and then they only take as tax an amount which would have gone to the federal government anyway.

The following states have estate or inheritance taxes, and they range as high as thirty-two percent. All of these exempt the spouse except Maryland and Mississippi. Some of them exempt smaller estates or children. If you have a large estate and live in one of these states, you should check with a tax advisor to see how much tax your estate or beneficiaries will have to pay.

States which have estate or inheritance taxes:

Connecticut	Mississippi	Ohio
Indiana	Montana	Oklahoma
Iowa	Nebraska	Pennsylvania
Kentucky	New Hampshire	South Dakota
Louisiana	New Jersey	Tennessee
Maryland	New York	

By setting up a primary residence in another state, you may be able to avoid estate taxes. However, remember that most states have income or capital gains taxes. States which have no income, capital gains, estate or inheritance taxes are Alaska, Florida, Nevada, Texas, Washington and Wyoming.

There are two things in which men, in other things wise enough, do usually miscarry; in putting off the making of their wills and their repentance until it is too late.
— Tillotson

DO YOU NEED A WILL?

WHAT A WILL CAN DO

BENEFICIARIES

A will allows you to decide who gets your property after your death. You can give specific personal items to certain persons and choose which of your friends or relatives, if any, deserve a greater share of your estate. You can also leave gifts to schools and charities.

EXECUTOR

A will allows you to decide who will be in charge of handling your estate. This is the person who gathers together all your assets and distributes them to the beneficiaries, hires attorneys or accountants if necessary, and files any essential tax or probate forms. In different states, this person may be called the *executor*, *personal representative*, or *administrator*. With a will, you can provide that your executor does not have to post a surety bond with the court in order to serve and this can save your estate some money. You can also give the executor the power to sell your property and take other actions without getting a court order.

GUARDIAN

A will allows you to choose a guardian for your minor children. This way, you can avoid fights among relatives and make sure the best person raises your children. You may also appoint separate guardians over your children and over their money. For example, you may appoint your sister as guardian over your children, and your father as guardian over their money. That way, a second person can keep an eye on how the children's money is being spent.

PROTECTING
HEIRS

You can set up a trust to provide that your property is not distributed immediately. Many people feel that their children would not be ready to handle large sums of money at the age of majority, which is eighteen in most states. A will can direct that the money is held until the children are twenty-one, twenty-five, or older.

MINIMIZING
TAXES

If your estate is over $675,000 (this amount will rise to $1,000,000 by 2006), it will be subject to federal estate taxes. If you wish to lower those taxes, by making gifts to charities for example, you can do so through a will. However, such estate planning is beyond the scope of this book and you should consult an estate planning attorney or another book for further information.

WHAT IF YOU HAVE NO WILL?

If you do not have a will, the *intestacy* laws of your state determine who gets your property. As explained earlier, any property you owned in joint tenancy would automatically go to the joint owner, and any property held in trust would go to the beneficiaries. (Subject to the spouse's share in some states.) But any property in your name alone would go to the persons named in your state's laws.

Each state's laws are different, but typically they provide as follows:

☛ If you have a spouse and children, the property is divided among them.

☛ If you have a spouse and parents or siblings but no children, some states give all to your spouse, but other states give your parents or siblings a share.

☛ If you have children but no spouse, your children get your property.

☛ If you have no children or spouse, your parents would get your property, except in a few states that give a share to your brothers and sisters.

☞ If you have no spouse, children, or parents, your brothers and sisters would share your property.

☞ If you have no spouse, children, parents, brothers, or sisters, your property would go to your grandparents, aunts and uncles, or nieces and nephews, in that order.

Keep in mind that the above are general rules and some states have slight variations on these distributions.

IS YOUR WILL STILL VALID IF YOU MOVE TO ANOTHER STATE?

A will that is valid in one state would probably be valid to pass property in another state. If your will is *self-proved*, as explained in the next chapter, it might be admitted to probate without delay. However, if the will is not self-proved, then the witnesses to your will would need to be found and their oath taken to validate your will. In some states, a person would need to be appointed to take the oath of the witness and this would add to the time and expense of probating your will. Because of this, it is advisable to execute a new will upon moving to another state.

Another advantage to having a new will is that it may help your estate avoid estate taxes in your former state.

EXAMPLE
☞ George and Barbara left their high-tax state and retired to Florida, which has no estate or inheritance taxes, but they never made a new will. Upon their deaths, their former state of residence tried to collect a tax from their estate because their old wills stated that they were residents of that state.

WHO CAN MAKE A WILL?

In most states, any person who is eighteen or more years of age, and of sound mind may make a will. However, in Georgia the age is fourteen, and in Louisiana, the age is sixteen.

In many states, a person who is married or in the armed forces is allowed to make a will even if he or she is under the legal age. If you are in either of these circumstances and wish to make a will, you should check with an attorney.

WHAT A WILL CANNOT DO

A will cannot direct that anything illegal be done and it cannot put unreasonable conditions on a gift. A provision that your daughter gets all of your property if she divorces her husband would be ignored by the court. She would get the property with no conditions attached. You can put some conditions in your will. You should consult with an attorney to be sure they are enforceable .

A will cannot leave money or property to an animal because animals cannot legally own property. If you wish to continue paying for care of an animal after your death, you should leave the funds in trust or to a friend whom you know will care for the animal.

WHO CAN USE A SIMPLE WILL

The wills in this book will pass your property whether your estate is $1,000 or $100,000,000. However, if your estate is over $675,000 (this amount will rise to $1,000,000 by 2006), you might be able to avoid estate taxes by using a trust or other tax-saving device. The larger your estate, the more you can save on estate taxes by doing more complicated planning. If you have a large estate and are concerned about estate taxes, you should consult an estate planning attorney or a book on estate planning.

WHO SHOULD NOT USE A SIMPLE WILL

WILL CONTEST
If you expect that there may be a fight over your estate or that someone might contest your will's validity, you should consult a lawyer. If you leave less than the statutory share of your estate to your spouse or if you leave one or more of your children out of your will, it is likely that someone will contest your will.

COMPLICATED ESTATES
If you are the beneficiary of a trust or have any complications in your legal relationships, you may need special provisions in your will.

BLIND OR UNABLE TO WRITE
A person who is blind or who can sign only with an "X" should also consult a lawyer about the proper way to make and execute a will.

ESTATES OVER $675,000
If you expect to have over $675,000 (this amount will rise to $1,000,000 by 2006) at the time of your death, then as discussed in the last section, you may want to consult with a CPA or tax attorney regarding tax consequences.

CONDITIONS
If you wish to put some sort of conditions or restrictions on the property you leave, you should consult a lawyer. For example, if you want to leave money to your brother only if he quits smoking, or to a hospital only if they name a wing in your honor, you should consult an attorney to be sure that your conditions are valid in your state.

What you leave at your death let it be without controversy, else the lawyers will be your heirs.
—F. Osborn

How to Make a Simple Will 3

Identifying Parties in Your Will

PEOPLE

When making your will, it is important to clearly identify the persons you name as your beneficiaries. In some families, names differ only by middle initial or by Jr. or Sr. Be sure to check everyone's name before making your will. You can also add your relationship to the beneficiary, and their location such as "my cousin, George Simpson of Clearwater, Florida."

ORGANIZATIONS

The same applies to organizations and charities. For example, there is more than one group using the words "cancer society" or "heart association" in their name. Be sure to get the correct name of the group to which you intend to leave your gift.

SPOUSE AND CHILDREN

In most states, you must mention your spouse and children in your will even if you do not leave them any property. That is to show that you are of sound mind and know who are your heirs. As mentioned earlier, if you have a spouse and/or children and plan to leave your property to persons other than them, you should consult an attorney to be sure that your will will be enforceable.

PERSONAL PROPERTY

Because people acquire and dispose of personal property so often, it is not advisable to list a lot of small items in your will. Otherwise, when you sell or replace one of them you may have to rewrite your will.

One solution is to describe the type of item you wish to give. For example, instead of saying, "I leave my 1998 Ford to my sister," you should say, "I leave any automobile I own at the time of my death to my sister."

Of course, if you do mean to give a specific item you should describe it. For example, instead of "I leave my diamond ring to Joan," you should say, "I leave to Joan the one-half carat diamond ring which I inherited from my grandmother," because you might own more than one diamond ring at the time of your death. (Hopefully!)

HANDWRITTEN LIST OF PERSONAL PROPERTY

In some states, you are allowed to leave a handwritten list of personal items that you wish to go to certain people and this would be legally binding. The states that allow this are listed in appendix A. If your state is listed you should make a handwritten list prior to making your will, sign and date it, and include the following statement under the "Specific Bequests" clause of your will.

> I may leave a statement or list disposing of certain items of my tangible personal property. Any such statement or list in existence at the time of my death shall be determinative with respect to all items bequeathed therein.

A handwritten note is not an option in most states. If you feel your family will honor your wishes, you can write out a list of personal items you want to go to certain people, but you must realize that there is no legal requirement for your list will be followed.

TAX NOTE

Section 663 of the Internal Revenue Code allows the exclusion of certain specific bequests of tangible personal property from the estate.

If your estate is over $675,000 (rising to $1,000,000 by 2006), you may want to consult a tax advisor about taking advantage of this provision.

SPECIFIC BEQUESTS

Occasionally, a person will want to leave a little something to a friend or charity and the rest to the family. This can be done with a *specific bequest* such as "$1,000 to my dear friend Martha Jones." Of course, there could be a problem if, at the time of a person's death, there wasn't anything left after the specific bequests.

EXAMPLE ☛ At the time of making his will, Todd had $1,000,000 in assets. He felt generous so he left $50,000 to a local hospital, $50,000 to a local group that took care of homeless animals, and the rest to his children. Unfortunately, several years later, the stock market crashed and he committed suicide by jumping off a bridge. His estate at the time was worth only $110,000 so after the above specific bequests and the legal fees and expenses of probate, there was nothing left for his five children.

Another problem with specific bequests is that some of the property may be worth considerably more or less at death than when the will was made.

EXAMPLE ☛ Joe wanted his two children to equally share his estate. His will left his son his stocks (worth $500,000 at the time) and his daughter $500,000 in cash. By the time of Joe's death the stock was only worth $100,000.

He should have left "fifty percent" of his estate to each child. If giving certain things to certain people is an important part of your estate plan, you can give specific items to specific persons, but remember to make changes if your assets change.

JOINT BENEFICIARIES

Be careful about leaving one item of personal property to more than one person. For example, if you leave something to your son and his wife, what would happen if they divorce? Even if you leave something to two of your own children, what if they can't agree about who will have possession of it? Whenever possible, leave property to one person.

REMAINDER CLAUSE

One of the most important clauses in a will is the *remainder clause* called a *residue clause* in some states. This is the clause that says something like "all the rest, residue, and remainder of my property I leave to…" This clause makes sure that the will disposes of all property owned at the time of death and that nothing is forgotten.

In a simple will, the best way to distribute property is to put it all in the remainder clause. In the first example in the previous section, the problem would have been avoided if the will had read as follows: "The rest, residue, and remainder of my estate I leave, five percent to ABC Hospital, five percent to XYZ Animal Welfare League and ninety percent to be divided equally among my children…"

ALTERNATE BENEFICIARIES

You should always provide for an *alternate beneficiary* in case the first one dies before you and you do not have a chance to make out a new will.

SURVIVORS OR DESCENDANTS

Suppose your will leaves your property to your sister and brother, but your brother predeceases you. Should his share go to your sister or to your brother's children or grandchildren?

If you are giving property to two or more persons and if you want it all to go to the other if one of them dies, then you would specify "or the survivor of them."

If, on the other hand, you want the property to go to the children of the deceased person, you should state in your will, "or their lineal descendants." This would include his or her children and grandchildren.

FAMILY OR
PERSON

If you decide you want it to go to your brother's children and grandchildren, you must next decide if an equal share should go to each family or to each person. For example, if your brother leaves three grandchildren, and one is an only child of his daughter and the others are the children of his son, should all grandchildren get equal shares, or should they take their parent's share?

When you want each family to get an equal share it is called *per stirpes*. When you want each person to get an equal share it is called *per capita*. Most of the wills in this book use per stirpes because that is the most common way property is left. If you wish to leave your property per capita, then you can rewrite the will with this change.

EXAMPLE

☛ Alice leaves her property to her two daughters, Mary and Pat in equal shares, or to their lineal descendants per stirpes. Both daughters die before Alice. Mary leaves one child; Pat leaves two children. In this case, Mary's child would get half of the estate and Pat's children would split the other half of the estate. If Alice had specified per capita instead of per stirpes, each child would have gotten one-third of the estate.

Per Stirpes Distribution

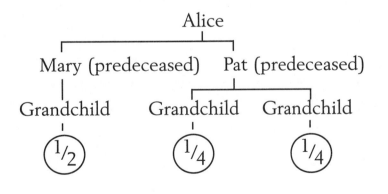

Per Capita Distribution

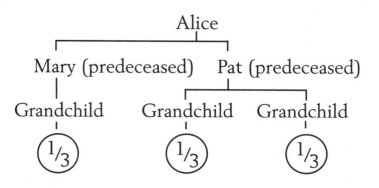

There are fourteen different will forms in this book that should cover the options most people want, but you may want to divide your property slightly differently from what is stated in these forms. If so, you can retype the forms according to these rules, specifying whether the property should go to the survivor or the lineal descendants. If this is confusing to you, you should consider seeking the advice of an attorney.

SURVIVORSHIP

Many people put a clause in their will stating that anyone receiving property under the will must survive for thirty days (or forty-five or sixty) after the death of the person who made the will. This is so that if the two people die in the same accident, there will not be two probates and the property will not go to the other party's heirs.

EXAMPLE

☛ Fred and Wilma were married and each had children by previous marriages. They didn't have survivorship clauses in their wills and they were in an airplane crash and died. Fred's children hired several expert witnesses and a large law firm to prove that at the time of the crash Fred lived for a few minutes longer than Wilma. That way, when Wilma died first, all of her property went to Fred. When he died a few minutes later, all of Fred and Wilma's property went to his children. Wilma's children got nothing.

GUARDIANS

If you have minor children, you should name a guardian for them. There are two types of guardians, a guardian over the *person* and a guardian over the *property*. The first is the person who decides where the children will live and makes the other parental decisions for them. A guardian of the property is in charge of the minor's property and inheritance. In most cases, one person is appointed guardian of both the person and property. But some people prefer that the children live with one person and that the money be held by another person.

EXAMPLE

☛ Sandra was a widow with a young daughter. She knew that if anything happened to her, her sister would be the best person to raise her daughter. But her sister was never good with money. So when Sandra made out her will, she named her sister as guardian over the person of her daughter and she named her father as guardian over the estate of her daughter.

When naming a guardian, it is always advisable to name an alternate guardian in case your first choice is unable to serve for any reason.

CHILDREN'S TRUST

When a parent dies leaving a minor child and the child's property is held by a guardian, the guardianship ends when the child reaches the age of eighteen, and all of the property is turned over to the child. Most parents do not feel their children are competent at the age of eighteen to handle large sums of money and prefer that it be held until the child is twenty-one, twenty-five, thirty, or even older.

If you wish to set up a complicated system of determining when your children should receive various amounts of your estate, or if you want the property held to a higher age than thirty-five, you should consult a lawyer to draft a trust. However, if you want a simple provision that the funds be held until they reach a higher age than eighteen, and you have someone you trust to make decisions about paying for education or other expenses for your child or children, you can put that provision in your will as a children's trust.

The children's trust trustee can be the same person as the guardian or a different person. It is advisable to name an alternate trustee if your first choice is unable to handle it.

Executor/Personal Representative

An *executor* (also called *personal representative* or *administrator* in some states) is the person who will be in charge of your probate. He or she will gather your assets, handle the sale of them if necessary, prepare an inventory, hire an attorney, and distribute the property. This should be a person you trust, and if it is, then you can state in your will that no bond will be required to be posted by him or her. Otherwise, the court will require that a surety bond be paid for by your estate to guaranty that the person is honest. You can appoint a bank to handle your estate but their fees are usually very high.

It is best to appoint a resident of your state for two reasons: one, it is easier; and two, a bond may be required of a non-resident even if your will waives it.

Some people like to name two persons to handle their estate to avoid jealousy, or to have them check on each other's honesty. However, this is not a good idea. It makes double work in getting the papers signed, and there can be problems if they cannot agree on something.

The person handling your estate is usually entitled to some compensation. Some states specify a percentage while others allow an hourly fee. A family member will often waive the fee, but if there is a lot of work involved he or she may request the fee, or other family members may insist that he or she take one. You can insist in your will that your executor/personal representative is paid a fee.

In most states, an executor or personal representative cannot sell real estate without approval by the court. If you trust your executor, you can avoid the expense and delay of this by giving him or her the power to do so without court approval.

WITNESSES

A will must be witnessed by two persons to be valid in all states except Vermont which requires three witnesses. Each state has its own rule as to who can be a competent witness. While some states allow minors to witness wills, you should be sure that both of your witnesses are over eighteen just to be safe.

The witnesses should not be people who are beneficiaries of your will. In about half the states, the witnesses *can* be beneficiaries; but it is even better in those states if they are not in case a question of undue influence arises.

SELF-PROVING AFFIDAVIT

A will only needs two witnesses to be legal (except in Vermont), but it is highly recommended in most states that you include a notarized *self-proving* affidavit to the will. This is usually a separate sheet attached to your will and it is signed and notarized at the same time your will is signed and witnessed.

If a will is accompanied by a notarized self-proving affidavit, it may be admitted to probate without delay and without further contacting the witnesses.

Without a self-proving affidavit, your will cannot be admitted to probate until the court determines that it is valid. This can mean the witnesses must be located and asked to sign an oath, or if the witnesses are dead, someone may have to verify your handwriting.

The list below will tell you if you can use a self-proving affidavit and if so, which one to use.

California, the District of Columbia, Michigan, and Wisconsin do not need to use these forms, and Ohio and Vermont do not provide for them.

Alabama	Form 17	Montana	Form 17
Alaska	Form 17	Nebraska	Form 17
Arizona	Form 17	Nevada	Form 17
Arkansas	Form 17	New Hampshire	Form 20
California	Not necessary	New Jersey	Form 18
Colorado	Form 17	New Mexico	Form 17
Connecticut	Form 17	New York	Form 17
Delaware	Form 18	North Carolina	Form 18
D. C.	Not necessary	North Dakota	Form 17
Florida	Form 18	Ohio	Not available
Georgia	Form 18	Oklahoma	Form 18
Hawaii	Form 17	Oregon	Form 17
Idaho	Form 17	Pennsylvania	Form 18
Illinois	Form 17	Rhode Island	Form 18
Indiana	Form 17	South Carolina	Form 17
Iowa	Form 18	South Dakota	Form 17
Kansas	Form 18	Tennessee	Form 17
Kentucky	Form 18	Texas	Form 21
Louisiana	Form 19	Utah	Form 17
Maine	Form 17	Vermont	Not available
Maryland	Not necessary	Virginia	Form 18
Massachusetts	Form 18	Washington	Form 17
Michigan	Not necessary	West Virginia	Form 17
Minnesota	Form 17	Wisconsin	Not necessary
Mississippi	Form 17	Wyoming	Form 18
Missouri	Form 18		

In an emergency situation, for example, if you are bedridden and there is no notary available, you can execute your will without the self-proving page. As long as it has two disinterested witnesses (three in Vermont), it will be valid. The only drawback is that at least one of the witnesses will later have to sign an oath.

DISINHERITING SOMEONE

Because it may result in your will being challenged in court, you should not make your own will if you intend to disinherit someone. However, you may wish to leave one child less than another because you already made a gift to that child, or perhaps that because child needs the money less than the other.

If you do give more to one child than to another, then you should state your reasons, in order to show that you thought out your plan. Otherwise, the one who received less might argue that you didn't realize what you were doing and were not competent to make a will.

FUNERAL ARRANGEMENTS

There is no harm in stating your preferences in your will, but in most states, directions for a funeral are not legally enforceable. A will is often not found until after the funeral. Therefore, it is better to tell your family about your wishes or to make prior arrangements yourself.

FORMS

There are several different forms included in this book for easy use. You can either cut them out or photocopy them, or you can retype them on plain paper.

HANDWRITTEN WILLS

In some states, you can hand write your own will, without any witnesses, and it will be held valid. This is called a *holographic* will. As a general rule, it must be completely hand written in your own handwriting, be dated and signed and clearly express your intention to make it your will. It is only valid in the states listed in appendix A.

Since there is a greater chance it may be held invalid for some reason, a holographic will should only be used if you are in an emergency situation and are unable to find anyone to sign as witnesses.

LOUISIANA

Louisiana's legal system is different from all forty-nine other states. This is because it is based on the French system rather than the English.

Under Louisiana law, there are two types of wills. The original will law required a will to be transcribed by a notary, witnessed by three persons (five if they do not reside locally), and strictly follow certain formalities.

Recently, Louisiana passed a statutory will law that is similar to most other states. A statutory will needs only two witnesses but it *must be notarized* and *every page must be signed in full by the testator*. For Louisiana, we have provided a notary page instead of a self-proved will page. Also, since Louisiana has parishes rather than counties, the word "County" should be crossed out and replaced with the word "Parish."

CAUTIONS

Your will should have no white-outs or erasure marks. If for some reason it is impossible to make a will without corrections, they should be initialed by you and both witnesses. The pages should be fastened together and they should state at the bottom, "page 1 of 3," "page 2 of 3," etc. If you are using a self-proved will page or notary page, you should include this page in the numbering of the pages to be sure it is counted as part of your will. Each page should be initialed by you and by the witnesses.

One eye-witness is worth more than ten who tell what they have heard.
—Plautus, c. 254 - 184 B.C.

How to Execute Your Will 4

The signing of a will is a serious legal event and must be done properly or the will may be declared invalid. Preferably, it should be done in a private room without distraction. All parties must watch each other sign and no one should leave the scene until all have signed.

EXAMPLE
☛ Ebenezer was bedridden in a small room. His will was brought in to him to sign, but the witnesses could not actually see his hand signing because a dresser was in the way. His will was ignored by the court and his property went to two persons who were not in his will.

To be sure your will is valid, you should follow these rules:

PROCEDURE
☛ You must state to your witnesses: "This is my will. I have read it and I understand it and this is how I want it to read. I want you two (or three) people to be my witnesses." Contrary to popular belief, you do not have to read it to the witnesses or to let them read it.

☛ You must date your will and sign your name at the end in ink exactly as it is printed in the will, and you should initial each page as both witnesses watch. In Louisiana, you must sign each page of the will with your full signature and have your will notarized.

☛ You and the other witnesses must watch as each witness signs in ink and initials each page.

SELF-PROVING
AFFIDAVIT

As explained in the last chapter, it is important to attach a self-proving affidavit to your will. This means that you will need to have a notary public present to watch everyone sign. If it is impossible to have a notary present, your will will still be valid (except in Louisiana), but the probate process may be delayed.

After your witnesses have signed as attesting witnesses under your name, you and they should sign the self-proving page and the notary should notarize it. The notary should not be one of your witnesses.

It is a good idea to make at least one copy of your will, but you should not personally sign the copies or have them notarized. The reason for this is if you cancel or destroy your will someone may produce a copy and have it probated; or if you lose or destroy a copy, a court may assume you intended to revoke the original.

EXAMPLE

☛ Michael typed out a copy of his will and made two photocopies. He had the original and both copies signed and notarized. He then gave the original to his sister who was his executor and kept the two copies. Upon his death the two copies were not found among his papers. Because these copies were in his possession and not found, it was assumed that he destroyed them. A court ruled that by destroying them, he must have intended to revoke the original will and his property went to persons not listed in his will.

AFTER YOU SIGN YOUR WILL 5

STORING YOUR WILL

Your will should be kept in a place safe from fire and easily accessible to your heirs. Your personal representative or executor should know of its whereabouts. It can be kept in a home safe or fire box.

In some states, the opening of a safe deposit box in a bank after a person's death is a complicated affair, so it is not advisable to keep it there.

If you are close to your children and can trust them explicitly, you could allow one of them to keep the will in his or her safe deposit box. However, if you later decide to limit that child's share there could be a problem.

EXAMPLE

☞ Diane made out her will giving her property to her two children equally and gave it to her older child, Bill, to hold. Years later, Bill moved away and her younger child, Mary, took care of her by coming over every day. Diane made a new will giving most her property to Mary. Upon Diane's death, Bill came to town and found the new will in Diane's house, but he destroyed it and probated the old will which gave him half the property.

In some states, a will can be filed with the probate division of the local court system. This can be a good way to be sure your will is not lost;

however, if you ever want to revoke your will while in the hospital, it could make things more difficult.

Revoking Your Will

The usual way to revoke a will is to execute a new one that states that it revokes all previously made wills. To revoke a will without making a new one, one can tear, burn, cancel, deface, obliterate, or destroy it, as long as this is done with the intention of revoking it. If this is done accidentally, the will is not legally revoked.

EXAMPLE
☞ Ralph tells his son Clyde to go to the basement safe and tear up his (Ralph's) will. If Clyde does not tear it up in Ralph's presence, it is probably not effectively revoked.

REVIVAL
What if you change your will by drafting a new one and later decide you don't like the changes and want to go back to your old will? Can you destroy the new one and revive the old one? NO! Once you execute a new will revoking an old will, you cannot revive the old will unless you execute a new document stating that you intend to revive the old will. In other words, you really should execute a new will.

Changing Your Will

You should not make any changes on your will after it has been signed. If you cross out a person's name or add a clause to a will that has already been signed, your change will not be valid and your entire will might become invalid.

One way to amend a will is to execute a *codicil*. A codicil is an amendment to a will. However, a codicil must be executed just like a will. It must have the same number of witnesses, and to be self-proved it must include a self-proving page that must be notarized.

Because a codicil requires the same formality as a will, it is usually better to just make a new will.

In an emergency situation, if you want to change something in your will, but cannot get to a notary to have it self-proved, you can execute a codicil which is witnessed, but not self-proved. As long as it is properly witnessed (two witnesses in all states except Vermont which requires three), it will legally change your will. The only drawback would be that the witnesses would have to later sign an oath if it were not self-proved.

To prepare a codicil in any state except Louisiana, use form 22. To self-prove the codicil, use forms 23, 24, or 25. See page 38 for a list of which form to use for which state.

HOW TO MAKE A LIVING WILL 6

No, a living will is not a videotape of a person making a will. It has nothing to do with the usual type of will that distributes property. A living will is a document by which a person declares that he or she does not want artificial life support systems used if he or she becomes terminally ill.

Modern science can often keep a body alive even if the brain is permanently dead, or if the person is in constant pain. In recent years, all states have legalized living wills either by statute or by court decision. Some states have suggested forms and others allow any writing that reasonably express a person's wishes.

A living will must be signed in front of two witnesses who should not be blood relatives or a spouse. If the person is physically unable to sign, he or she may read the living will out loud and direct one of the witnesses to sign it for him or her.

A living will form is included in appendix C of this book. This form complies with the law in every state. However, some doctors are more comfortable with the form designed for their state, even if it is not required. If you wish to use your state's form, you can probably get one from your doctor or hospital, or you can consult the book, *How to Write Your Own Living Will*, by Edward A. Haman.

Behold, I do not give lectures or a little charity, When I give I give myself.
—Walt Whitman, Leaves of Grass

HOW TO MAKE ANATOMICAL GIFTS 7

Residents of all states are allowed to donate their bodies or organs for research or transplantation. Consent may be given by a relative of a deceased person, but because relatives are often in shock or too upset to make such a decision, it is better to have one's intent made clear before death. This can be done by a statement in a will or by another signed document such as a Uniform Donor Card. The gift may be of all or part of one's body, and it may be made to a specific person such as a physician or an ill relative.

The document making the donation must be signed before two witnesses who must also sign in each other's presence. If the donor cannot sign, then the document may be signed for him at his direction in the presence of the witnesses.

The donor may designate in the document who the physician is that will carry out the procedure.

If the document or will has been delivered to a specific donee it may be amended or revoked by the donor in the following ways:

- ☛ By executing and delivering a signed statement to the donee.
- ☛ By an oral statement to two witnesses communicated to the donee.
- ☛ By an oral statement made to an attending physician during a terminal illness and communicated to the donee.

☞ By a signed document found on the person of the donor or in his or her effects.

If a document of gift has not been delivered to a donee, it may be revoked by any of the above methods or by destruction, cancellation, or mutilation of the document. It may also be revoked in the same method a will is revoked as described on page 44.

A Uniform Donor Card is included in appendix C as form 27. It must be signed in the presence of two signing witnesses.

GLOSSARY

In order to make a will, you should understand the legal terms which are used in estate planning and probate.

administrator (if female, sometimes called **administratrix**): a person appointed by a court to manage a person's state (for example, if no executor was named).

beneficiary: a person who is left property in a will.

bequeath: to leave someone personal property in a will.

bequest: a gift of personal property in a will.

codicil: an amendment to a will.

decedent: a person who has died.

descendant: a child, grandchild, great-grandchild, etc.

devise: a gift of real property in a will; also to leave real property in a will

devisee: a person who is left real property in a will

elective share: the amount of property a spouse can claim even if nothing was left to him or her in the will.

executor (if female, sometimes called **executrix**): a person appointed in a will to manage a decedent's estate. In some states, this person is now called a personal representative.

exempt property: property regularly used by decedent's family and that is not considered part of the estate.

family allowance: an amount allowed by law to the spouse and children of a decedent.

forced share: see *elective share* above.

heir: a person who inherits property from a person without a will.

homestead: in some states, the residence of a person who is married or has minor children.

intestate: the state of dying without a valid will.

intestate share: the amount of property an heir receives from the estate of a person who died without a will.

joint tenancy (sometimes called **joint tenancy with right of survivorship**): ownership of property in which, upon death, an owner's share goes to the other joint owner.

legacy: a gift of personal property in a will.

living will: a document which directs medical personnel whether or not to use extraordinary measures to keep a body alive after certain life functions have ceased.

personal representative: a person appointed in a will to manage a decedent's estate. In some states this person is now called an executor.

POD (also **P/O/D**): pay on death, usually used on bank accounts and in some states on securities.

probate: the procedure of gathering a decedent's assets and distributing them to the heirs or beneficiaries

remainder: balance of an estate after all specific gifts have been distributed.

residue: balance of an estate after all specific gifts have been distributed.

specific bequest: the gift of a specific item of personal property to a specific person in a will.

specific devise: the gift of a specific parcel of real property to a specific person in a will.

tenancy by the entireties: in some states, the ownership of property by a husband and wife as one entity. When one dies the other still owns the entire property.

tenancy in common: ownership of property in which, upon death, each owner's share goes to his or her heirs or beneficiaries.

testate: to be with a valid will, as in "a testate estate."

testator: a person making a will.

TOD (also **T/O/D**): transfer on death. Usually used on bank accounts and in some states on securities.

Totten trust: tilting property "in trust for" another person, but which can be changed at any time before death.

Appendix A
State Laws

Since the laws are different in each state, the following tables have been included to provide information about your specific state on matters discussed in the text. Keep in mind that laws are amended frequently and are subject to different interpretations by different courts.

Spouse's Entitlement to Estate

The following table is a summary of the share of an estate that a spouse is entitled to by law. Where only a fraction or percentage is given the share is of the probatable estate, when the word *augmented* is used it means all assets passing at death are used to calculate the share. Where the word *community* is used the state is a community property state and the spouse is entitled to one-half of all community property which is most property acquired during the marriage. Where it says "up to fifty percent," this is usually a sliding scale based on the length of the marriage.

Keep in mind that these are brief summaries and that the laws can change. If this is an issue in your estate planning, check the most recent version of your state statute or consult an attorney.

State	Share	Statute
Alabama	¹/₃ augmented	C.A. § 43-8-70
Alaska	¹/₃ augmented	A.S. § 13.12.201-.214
Arizona	¹/₂ community	A.R.S. § 25-211
Arkansas	¹/₃ to ¹/₂	A.C.A. § 11-301, 305, 307
California	¹/₂ community	A.C.C. Probate § 6560
Colorado	5% to 50% augmented	C.R.S.A. § 15-11-201
Connecticut	¹/₃ for life	C.G.S.A. § 45A-436
Delaware	¹/₃ augmented	D.C.A. 12 §§ 901 TO 908
D. C.	¹/₃ up to ¹/₂	D.C.C. § 19-113(e)
Florida	30% augmented	F.S. § 732.201, 732.2065
Georgia	one year's support	C.G.A. § 53-3-13
Hawaii	up to 50% augmented	H.R.S. § 560:2-201
Idaho	¹/₂ augmented quasi-community	I.C. § 15-2-203
Illinois	¹/₂ if no children. ¹/₃ if children	755 ILCS 5/2-8
Indiana	¹/₂ if no children. ¹/₃ if children	A.I.C. § 29-1-3-1
Iowa	¹/₃ plus all exempt	I.C.A. § 633.238
Kansas	up to 50% augmented	K.S.A. § 59-6a202
Kentucky	¹/₂ pers. prop., ¹/₃ real estate	K.R.S. § 392.020 and -.080
Louisiana	¹/₂ community	
Maine	¹/₃ augmented	18a M.R.S.A. §§ 2-201
Maryland	¹/₂ if no children, ¹/₃ if children	A.C.M. Est. & Tr. § 3-203
Massachusetts	$25k + ¹/₂ w/o ch, ¹/₃ if children	A.L.M. C.191 § 15

Michigan	½ of intstate	M.S.A. § 27.5282; M.C.L.A. § 700.282
Minnesota	up to 50%	M.S.A. § 524.2-202
Mississippi	½	M.C. §§ 91-1-7; 91-5-25; 91-5-27
Missouri	½ if no children. ⅓ if children	A.M.S. § 474-160
Montana	up to 50% augmented	M.C.A. § 72-2-221
Nebraska	½ augmented	R.S.N. § 30-2313
Nevada	½ community + support	N.R.S. § 146.010
New Hampshire	½ +$10K w/o ch., ⅓ if ch.	N.H.R.S.A. § 560:10
New Jersey	⅓ augmented	N.J.S.A. § 3B:8-1
New Mexico	½ community	
New York	½ if no children. ⅓ if children	C.L.N.Y., E.P.&Tr. § 5-1.1(c)
North Carolina	¼ to ½	G.S.N.C. §§ 29-14 and 30-1
North Dakota	½ augmented?	N.D.C.C. § 30.1-05-01
Ohio	½ if no or 1 child. ⅓ if 2 ch.	O.R.C. § 2106.01
Oklahoma	½ marital property	84 O.S.A. § 44
Oregon	½ community	O.R.S. § 112.705 -.775
Pennsylvania	⅓ augmented	20 Pa. C.S.A. § 2203
Rhode Island	⅓ real estate for life + $75,000	G.L.R.I. §§ 33-1-6, 33-25-2
South Carolina	⅓	C.L.S.C. § 62-2-201
South Dakota	up to 50% augmented	S.D.C.L. § 29A-2-202
Tennessee	10% to 40%	T.C.A. § 31-4-101
Texas	½ community	Texas Constitution § 15
Utah	⅓ augmented	U.C.A. § 75-2-202
Vermont	⅓ or more	V.S.A. §§ 401 and 402
Virginia	½ if no children. ⅓ if children	C.V. § 64.1-16
Washington	½ community	
West Virginia	up to 50% augmented	W.V.C. § 42-3-1
Wisconsin	½ community	W.S.A. § 851.001
Wyoming	½ if no children of prior spouse ¼ if children of prior spouse	W.S.A. § 2-5-101

STATE STATUTES ALLOWING TRANSFERS AT DEATH OF SECURITIES

The following states allow securities to be registered in *Transfer-on-Death* form. If your state is listed you can ask that your stock and mutual fund accounts be set up in transfer-on-death format (see page 14).

If your state is not listed, check with your broker, lawyer or state statutes to see if your state's law has changed recently, or you can move your accounts to a company in a state which has passed the law.

Alabama	A. C. §§ 8-6-140 to 8-6-151
Alaska	A.S. 13.06.050, 13.33.301 to 13.33.310
Arizona	A.R.S. §§ 14-1201, 14-6301 to 14-6311
Arkansas	A.C.A. §§ 28-14-101 to 28-14-112
California	Probate Code §§ 5500 to 5512
Colorado	C.R.S.A. §§ 15-10-201, 15-15-301 to 15-15-311
Connecticut	C.G.S. §§ 45a-468 to 45a-468m
Delaware	12 Del. C. §§ 801 to 812
Florida	F.S. §§ 711.50 to 711.512
Hawaii	H.R.S. §§ 539-1 to 539-12
Idaho	I.C. §§ 15-6-301 to 16-6-312
Illinois	S.H.A. 815 ILCS 10/0.01 to 10/12
Indiana	I. C. §§ 32-4-1.6-1 to 32-4-1.6-15
Iowa	I. C. §§ 633.800 to 633.811
Kansas	K.S.A. 17-49a 01 to 17-49a 12
Kentucky	K. S. 292.6501 to 292.6512
Maine	18A M.R.A. §§ 6-301 to 6-312
Maryland	Code, Estates and Trusts, §§ 16-101 to 16-112
Massachusetts	M.G.L. c. 201E, §§ 101 to 402
Michigan	M.C.L.A. §§ 451.471 to 451.481
Minnesota	M.S.A. §§ 542.1-201, 524.6-301 to 524.6-311
Mississippi	Code §§ 91-21-1 to 91-21-25
Montana	M.C.A. §§ 72-1-103, 72-6-301 to 72-6-311
Nebraska	R.R.S. 1943, §§ 30-2209, 30-2734 to 30-2746
Nevada	Statutes §§ 111.480 to 111.650
New Hampshire	R.S. §§ 563-C:1 to 563-C:12

New Jersey	N.J.S.A. 3B:30-1 to3B:30-12
New Mexico	N.M.S.A. 1978, §§ 45-1-201, 45-6-301 to 45-6-311
North Dakota	N.D.C.C. 30.1-01-06, 30.1-31-21 to 30.1-31-30
Ohio	R.C. §§ 1709.01 to 1709.11
Oklahoma	71 Okl.St.Ann. §§ 901 to 913
Oregon	O.R.S. 59.535 to 59.585
Pennsylvania	20 Pa. C. S. §§ 6401 to 6413
Rhode Island	Gen. laws. §§ 7-11.1-1 to 7-11.1-12
South Carolina	Code §§ 35-6-10 to 35-6-100
South Dakota	S.C.D.L. 29A-6-301 to 29A-6-311
Utah	U.C.A. 1953, 75-6-301 to 75-6-313
Virginia	Code 1950, §§ 64.1-206.1 to 64.1-206.8
Washington	R.C.W.A. 21.35.005 to 21.35.901
West Virginia	Code, 36-10-1 to 36-10-12
Wisconsin	W.S.A. 705.21 to 705.30
Wyoming	W.S. 1977, §§ 2-16-101 to 2-16-112

STATES IN WHICH A WILL IS REVOKED BY MARRIAGE

In the following states, a will is revoked by marriage of the person making the will unless the person mentioned the intended spouse in the will.

Alabama
Alaska
Arizona
California
Colorado
Connecticut
D.C.
Florida
Georgia
Hawaii
Idaho
Iowa
Kansas
Kentucky
Maine
Maryland
Massachusetts
Michigan
Minnesota
Montana
Nevada
New Hampshire   [if there has been a child]
Oklahoma   [if there has been a child]
Oregon
Pennsylvania
Rhode Island
South Dakota
Tennessee   [if there has been a child]
Washington
West Virginia
Wisconsin

STATES IN WHICH A HANDWRITTEN LIST OF PERSONAL PROPERTY MAY BE USED WITH A WILL

In the following states, a person may write out a list of personal property by hand and the list must be honored if referred to in the will. It should be completely handwritten, dated prior to the date of the will and signed in ink.

Alaska*
Arizona*
Arkansas
California
Colorado*
Florida*
Hawaii*
Idaho*
Kentucky
Louisiana
Maine*
Michigan*
Minnesota*
Mississippi
Montana*
Nebraska*

Nevada
New Jersey
New Mexico*
North Carolina*
North Dakota*
Oklahoma
Pennsylvania
South Carolina
South Dakota*
Tennessee
Texas
Utah*
Virginia
West Virginia
Wyoming

*These states have specific statutes on tangible property clauses. In the others it is legal because they allow handwritten wills.

STATES IN WHICH A HANDWRITTEN WILL IS LEGAL WITHOUT WITNESSES

In the following states, a will that is completely handwritten, signed, and dated by the testator is valid even if it not witnessed. However, it must be completely handwritten, with the complete date and the testator's signature.

Alaska
Arizona
Arkansas
California
Colorado
Hawaii
Idaho
Kentucky
Louisiana
Maine
Michigan
Mississippi
Montana
Nebraska
Nevada
New Jersey
North Carolina
North Dakota
Oklahoma
Pennsylvania
South Dakota
Tennessee
Texas
Utah
Virginia
West Virginia
Wyoming

APPENDIX B
SAMPLE FILLED-IN FORMS

The following pages include sample filled-in forms for some of the wills in this book. They are filled out in different ways for different situations. You should look at all of them to see how the different sections can be completed.

Only one example of a self-proved will affidavit is shown, although you are advised to use this page in all states that allow it.

Last Will and Testament

I, _____John Smith_____ a resident of _____Dade_____
County, _Florida_____ do hereby make, publish, and declare this to be my Last Will and Testament, hereby revoking any and all Wills and Codicils heretofore made by me.

FIRST: I direct that all my just debts and funeral expenses be paid out of my estate as soon after my death as is practicable.

SECOND: I give, devise, and bequeath the following specific gifts:
I may leave a statement or list disposing of certain items of my tangible
personal property. Any such statement or list in existence at the time of my
death shall be determinative with respect to all items bequeathed therein.-----
----

[Note: This clause is only legal in
certain states, see appendix A.]

THIRD: I give, devise, and bequeath all my estate, real, personal, and mixed, of whatever kind and wherever situated, of which I may die seized or possessed, or in which I may have any interest or over which I may have any power of appointment or testamentary disposition, to my spouse, _____Barbara Smith_____. If my said spouse does not survive me, I give, and bequeath the said property to _____my sisters, Jan Smith, Joan Smith, and Jennifer Smith in equal shares_____
_____,
or the survivor of them.

FOURTH: In the event that any beneficiary fails to survive me by thirty days, then this will shall take effect as if that person had predeceased me.

FIFTH: I hereby nominate, constitute, and appoint _Barbara Smith_____ as Executor of this, my Last Will and Testament. In the event that such named person is unable or unwilling to serve at any time or for any reason, then I nominate, constitute, and appoint _____Reginald Smith_____ as Executor in the place and stead of the person first named herein. It is my will and I direct that my Executor shall not be required to furnish a bond for the faithful performance of his or her duties in any jurisdiction, any provision of law to the contrary notwithstanding, and I give my Executor full power to administer my estate, including the power to settle claims, pay debts, and sell, lease or exchange real and personal property without court order.

IN WITNESS WHEREOF I declare this to be my Last Will and Testament and execute it willingly as my free and voluntary act for the purposes expressed herein and I am of legal age and

Initials: ___JS___ ___BJ___ ___JD___ _____ Page _1_ of __2__
Testator   Witness   Witness   Witness

64

sound mind and make this under no constraint or undue influence, this ___29th___ day of
___January___, 20 _02_ at ___Miami Beach___ State of ___Florida___.

_____John Smith_____ L.S.

The foregoing instrument was on said date subscribed at the end thereof by
_____John Smith_____, the above named Testator who signed, published, and declared this instrument to be his/her Last Will and Testament in the presence of us and each of us, who thereupon at his/her request, in his/her presence, and in the presence of each other, have hereunto subscribed our names as witnesses thereto. We are of sound mind and proper age to witness a will and understand this to be his/her will, and to the best of our knowledge testator is of legal age to make a will, of sound mind, and under no constraint or undue influence.

_____Brenda Jones_____ residing at_____West Palm Beach, Florida_____

_____John Doe_____ residing at_____Key Largo, Florida_____

_____ residing at_____

Last Will and Testament

I, _____John Smith_____ a resident of ___Tioga___
County, ___New York___ do hereby make, publish, and declare this to be my Last Will
and Testament, hereby revoking any and all Wills and Codicils heretofore made by me.

FIRST: I direct that all my just debts and funeral expenses be paid out of my estate as soon
after my death as is practicable.

SECOND: I give, devise, and bequeath the following specific gifts:
I leave my 1999 GT Celica to my daughter Beamy Smith. I leave my entire coin
collection to my daughter Seamy Smith. I leave my Chris Craft boat and trail-
er to my daughter Amy. In the event my said daughters predecease me, said gifts
shall be part of the residue of my estate. --------------------------------

THIRD: I give, devise, and bequeath all my estate, real, personal, and mixed, of whatever
kind and wherever situated, of which I may die seized or possessed, or in which I may have any
interest or over which I may have any power of appointment or testamentary disposition, to my
spouse, ___Barbara Smith___. If my said spouse does not survive me,
I give, and bequeath the said property to my children ___Amy Smith, Beamy Smith, and
Seamy Smith___

___
in equal shares or to their lineal descendants, per stirpes.

FOURTH: In the event that any beneficiary fails to survive me by thirty days, then this will
shall take effect as if that person had predeceased me.

FIFTH: I hereby nominate, constitute, and appoint ___Barbara Smith___ as
Executor of this, my Last Will and Testament. In the event that such named person is unable or
unwilling to serve at any time or for any reason, then I nominate, constitute, and appoint
___Reginald Smith___ as Executor in the place and stead of the person first named
herein. It is my will and I direct that my Executor shall not be required to furnish a bond for the
faithful performance of his or her duties in any jurisdiction, any provision of law to the contrary
notwithstanding, and I give my Executor full power to administer my estate, including the power to
settle claims, pay debts, and sell, lease or exchange real and personal property without court order.

IN WITNESS WHEREOF I declare this to be my Last Will and Testament and execute it
willingly as my free and voluntary act for the purposes expressed herein and I am of legal age and

Initials: ___JS___ ___BJ___ ___JD___ _____ Page _1_ of _2_
        Testator   Witness   Witness   Witness

66

sound mind and make this under no constraint or undue influence, this ___5th___ day of
___January___, 20_01_ at _____Owego_____ State of _____New York_____.

_____John Smith_____L.S.

The foregoing instrument was on said date subscribed at the end thereof by
_____John Smith_____, the above named Testator who signed, published, and declared this instrument to be his/her Last Will and Testament in the presence of us and each of us, who thereupon at his/her request, in his/her presence, and in the presence of each other, have hereunto subscribed our names as witnesses thereto. We are of sound mind and proper age to witness a will and understand this to be his/her will, and to the best of our knowledge testator is of legal age to make a will, of sound mind, and under no constraint or undue influence.

_____Brenda Jones_____residing at_____Oswego, New York_____

_____John Doe_____residing at_____Ithaca, New York_____

_____residing at_____

Last Will and Testament

I, _____John Doe_____ a resident of _____Fairfax_____ County, _____Virginia_____ do hereby make, publish, and declare this to be my Last Will and Testament, hereby revoking any and all Wills and Codicils heretofore made by me.

FIRST: I direct that all my just debts and funeral expenses be paid out of my estate as soon after my death as is practicable.

SECOND: I give, devise, and bequeath the following specific gifts:
_____-NONE-_____

THIRD: I give, devise, and bequeath all my estate, real, personal, and mixed, of whatever kind and wherever situated, of which I may die seized or possessed, or in which I may have any interest or over which I may have any power of appointment or testamentary disposition, to my children _____James Doe, Mary Doe, Larry Doe, Barry Doe, Carrie Doe, and Moe Doe._____

plus any afterborn or adopted children in equal shares or to their lineal descendants per stirpes.

FOURTH: In the event that any beneficiary fails to survive me by thirty days, then this will shall take effect as if that person had predeceased me.

FIFTH: In the event any of my children have not attained the age of 18 years at the time of my death, I hereby nominate, constitute, and appoint _____Herbert Doe_____ as guardian over the person of any of my children who have not reached the age of majority at the time of my death. In the event that said guardian is unable or unwilling to serve, then I nominate, constitute, and appoint _____Tom Doe_____ as guardian. Said guardian shall serve without bond or surety.

SIXTH: In the event any of my children have not attained the age of 18 years at the time of my death, I hereby nominate, constitute, and appoint _____Herbert Doe_____ as guardian over the property of any of my children who have not reached the age of majority at the time of my death. In the event that said guardian is unable or unwilling to serve, then I nominate, constitute, and appoint _____Tom Doe_____ as guardian. Said guardian shall serve without bond or surety.

Initials: ___JD___ ___JR___ ___MC___ _____ Page _1_ of _3_
Testator   Witness   Witness   Witness

SEVENTH: I hereby nominate, constitute, and appoint ___Clarence Doe___
as Executor of this, my Last Will and Testament. In the event that such named person is unable or unwilling to serve at any time or for any reason, then I nominate, constitute, and appoint ___Englebert Doe___ as Executor in the place and stead of the person first named herein. It is my will and I direct that my Executor shall not be required to furnish a bond for the faithful performance of his or her duties in any jurisdiction, any provision of law to the contrary notwithstanding, and I give my Executor full power to administer my estate, including the power to settle claims, pay debts, and sell, lease or exchange real and personal property without court order.

IN WITNESS WHEREOF I declare this to be my Last Will and Testament and execute it willingly as my free and voluntary act for the purposes expressed herein and I am of legal age and sound mind and make this under no constraint or undue influence, this _2nd_ day of _July_____, 20_00_ at _Fairfax_____ State of _Virginia_____.

_____John Doe_____L.S.

The foregoing instrument was on said date subscribed at the end thereof by _____John Doe_____, the above named Testator who signed, published, and declared this instrument to be his/her Last Will and Testament in the presence of us and each of us, who thereupon at his/her request, in his/her presence, and in the presence of each other, have hereunto subscribed our names as witnesses thereto. We are of sound mind and proper age to witness a will and understand this to be his/her will, and to the best of our knowledge testator is of legal age to make a will, of sound mind, and under no constraint or undue influence.

_____Jane Roe_____residing at___Falls Church, Virginia_____

_____Melvin Coe_____residing at___Burke, Virginia_____

_____residing at_____

Self-Proved Will Affidavit
(attach to Will)

STATE OF ___North Carolina___

COUNTY OF ___Onslow___

    I, the undersigned, an officer authorized to administer oaths, certify that _____John Doe_____, the testator and ___Jane Roe___, and ___Melvin Coe___, the witnesses, whose names are signed to the attached or foregoing instrument and whose signatures appear below, having appeared before me and having been first been duly sworn, each then declared to me that: 1) the attached or foregoing instrument is the last will of the testator; 2) the testator willingly and voluntarily declared, signed, and executed the will in the presence of the witnesses; 3) the witnesses signed the will upon the request of the testator, in the presence and hearing of the testator and in the presence of each other; 4) to the best knowledge of each witness, the testator was, at the time of signing, of the age of majority (or otherwise legally competent to make a will), of sound mind and memory, and under no constraint or undue influence; and 5) each witness was and is competent and of proper age to witness a will.

_____*John Doe*_____ (Testator)

_____*Jane Roe*_____ (Witness)

_____*Melvin Coe*_____ (Witness)

Subscribed and sworn to before me by _____John Doe_____, the testator, who is personally known to me or who has produced ___*___ as identification, and by ___Jane Roe___, a witness, who is personally known to me or who has produced ___*___ as identification, and by ___Melvin Coe___, a witness, who is personally known to me or who has produced ___*___ as identification, this __5th__ day of_____July_____, 20__03__.

> * Note: Identification is not required in every state.

_____*C.U. Sine*_____
Notary or other officer

Page _3_ of _3_

First Codicil to the Will of

_____ Larry Lowe _____

I, _____ Larry Lowe _____, a resident of _____ Broome _____ County, _____ New York _____ declare this to be the first codicil to my Last Will and Testament dated _____ July 5 _____, _ 1999 .

FIRST: I hereby revoke the clause of my Will which reads as follows: FOURTH: I hereby leave $5000.00 to my daughter Mildred----------------------

----

--.

SECOND: I hereby add the following clause to my Will: -------------------------
FOURTH: I hereby leave $1000.00 to my daughter Mildred

--.

THIRD: In all other respects I hereby confirm and republish my Last Will and Testament dated _____ July 5 _____, _ 1999 .

IN WITNESS WHEREOF, I have signed, published, and declared the foregoing instrument as and for a codicil to my Last Will and Testament, this __ 5th __ day of ___ January ___, 20 00 .

_____ *Larry Lowe* _____

The foregoing instrument was on the 5th day of ___ January ___, 2000 , signed at the end thereof, and at the same time published and declared by _____ Larry Lowe _____, as and for a codicil to his/~~her~~ Last Will and Testament, dated _____ July 5 _____, _ 1999 , in the presence of each of us, who, this attestation clause having been read to us, did at the request of the said testator/~~testatrix~~, in his/~~her~~ presence and in the presence of each other signed our names as witnesses thereto.

_ *James Smith* _ residing at_____ Binghamton, New York _____

_ *Mary Smith* _ residing at_____ Elmira, New York _____

_____ residing at_____

APPENDIX C
FORMS

The following pages contain forms that can be used to prepare a will, codicil, living will, and Uniform Donor Card. They should only be used by persons who have read this book, who do not have any complications in their legal affairs and who understand the forms they are using. The forms may be used right out of the book or they may be photocopied or retyped. Two copies of each form are included.

Form 1. Asset and Beneficiary List—*Use this form to keep an accurate record of your estate as well as your beneficiaries' names and addresses.*

Form 2. Preferences and Information List—*Use this form to let your family know of your wishes on matters not usually included in a will.*

Form 3. Simple Will—Spouse and Minor Children—One Guardian. *Use this will if you have minor children and want all your property to go to your spouse, but if your spouse dies previously, then to your minor children. It provides for one person to be guardian over your children and their estates.*

Form 4. Simple Will—Spouse and Minor Children—Two Guardians. *Use this will if you have minor children and want all your property to go to your spouse, but if your spouse dies previously, then to your minor children. It provides for two guardians, one over your children and one over their estates.*

Form 5. Simple Will—Spouse and Minor Children—Guardian and Trust. *This will should be used if you have minor children and want all your property to go to your spouse, but if your spouse dies previously, then to your minor children. It provides for one person to be guardian over your children and for either the same person or another to be trustee over their property. This will allows* *your children's property to be held until they are older than 18 rather than distributing it all to them at age 18.*

Form 6. Simple Will—Spouse and no children. *Use this will if you want your property to go to your spouse but if your spouse predeceases you, to others or the **survivor** of the others.*

Form 7. Simple Will—Spouse and no children. *Use this will if you want your property to go to your spouse but if your spouse predeceases you, to others or the **descendants** of the others.*

Form 8. Simple Will—Spouse and Adult Children. *Use this will if you want all of your property to go to your spouse, but if your spouse dies previously, then to your children, all of whom are adults.*

Form 9. Simple Will—Spouse and Adult Children. *Use this will if you want some of your property to go to your spouse, and some of your property to your children, all of whom are adults.*

Form 10. Simple Will—No Spouse—Minor Children—One Guardian. *Use this will if you do not have a spouse and want all your property to go to your children, at least one of whom is a minor. It provides for one person to be guardian over your children and their estates.*

Form 11. Simple Will—No Spouse—Minor Children—Two Guardians. *Use this will if you do not have a spouse and want all your property to go to your children, at least one of whom is a minor. It provides for two guardians, one over your children and one over their estates.*

Form 12. Simple Will—No Spouse—Minor Children—Guardian and Trust. *Use this will if you do not have a spouse and want all your property to go to your children, at least one of whom is a minor. It provides for one person to be guardian over your children and for either that person or another to be trustee over their property. This will allows your children's property to be held until they are older than 18 rather than distributing it all to them at age 18.*

Form 13. Simple Will—No Spouse—Adult Children. *This will should be used if you wish to leave your property to your adult children, or equally to each **family** if they predecease you.*

Form 14. Simple Will—No Spouse—Adult Children. *This will should be used if you wish to leave your property to your adult children, or equally to each **person** if they predecease you.*

Form 15. Simple Will—No spouse and no children. *Use this will if you have no spouse or children and want your property to go to the **survivor** of the people you name.*

Form 16. Simple Will—No spouse and no children. *Use this will if you have no spouse or children and want your property to go to the **descendants** of the people you name.*

Form 17. Self-Proved Will Page. *This affidavit should be used with the will if you live in Alabama, Alaska, Arizona, Arkansas, Colorado, Connecticut, Hawaii, Idaho, Illinois, Indiana, Maine, Minnesota, Mississippi, Montana, Nebraska, Nevada, New Mexico, New York, North Dakota, Oregon, South Carolina, South Dakota, Tennessee, Utah, Washington, or West Virginia.*

Form 18. Self-Proved Will Page. *This affidavit should be used with the will if you live in Delaware, Florida, Georgia, Iowa, Kansas, Kentucky, Massachusetts, Missouri, New Jersey, North Carolina, Oklahoma, Pennsylvania, Rhode Island, Virginia, Wyoming.*

Form 19. Notarized Will Page. *This affidavit should be used with the will if you live in Louisiana.*

Form 20. Self-Proved Will Page. *This affidavit should be used with the will if you live in New Hampshire.*

Form 21. Self-Proved Will Page. *This affidavit should be used with the will if you live in Texas.*

Form 22. Codicil to Will. *This form can be used to change one section of your will. Usually it is just as easy to execute a new will, since all of the same formalities are required. This codicil cannot be used in Louisiana.*

Form 23. Self-Proved Codicil Page. *If you decided to execute a codicil instead of making a new will, this page should be attached to your codicil if you live in Alabama, Alaska, Arizona, Arkansas, Colorado, Connecticut, Hawaii, Idaho, Illinois, Indiana, Maine, Minnesota, Mississippi, Montana, Nebraska, Nevada, New Mexico, New York, North Dakota, Oregon, South Carolina, South Dakota, Tennessee, Utah, Washington, or West Virginia.*

Form 24. Self-Proved Codicil Page. *If you decided to execute a codicil instead of making a new will, this page should be attached to your codicil if you live in Delaware, Florida, Georgia, Iowa, Kansas, Kentucky, Massachusetts, Missouri, New Jersey, North Carolina, Oklahoma, Pennsylvania, Rhode Island, Virginia, Wyoming.*

Form 25. Self-Proved Codicil Page. *If you decided to execute a codicil instead of making a new will, this affidavit should be used with the will if you live in Texas.*

Form 26. Living Will. *This is a document which expresses your desire to withhold certain extraordinary medical treatment should you have a terminal illness and you reach such a state that your wishes to withhold such treatment cannot be determined.*

Form 27. Organ Donor Card. *This form is used to spell out your wishes for donation of your body or any organs.*

How to Pick the Right Will

Follow the chart and use the form number in the black circle, then use the affidavit in the black box.

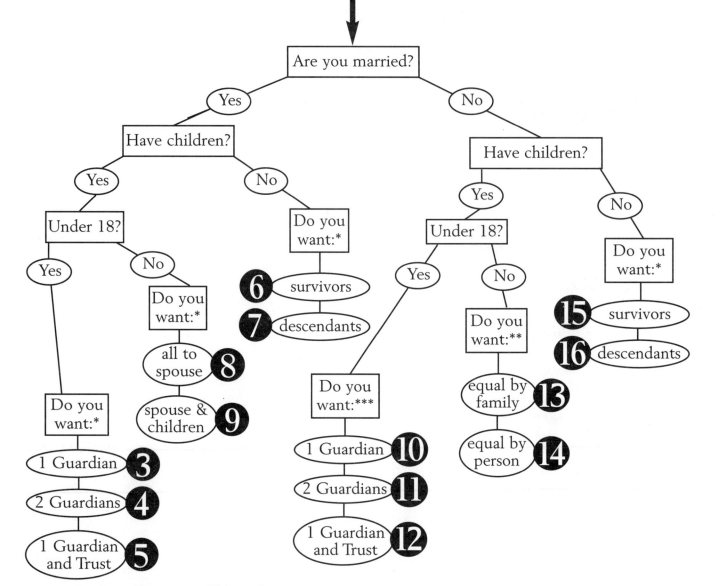

Use the self-proving affidavit for your state:

17 Alabama, Alaska, Arizona, Arkansas, Colorado, Connecticut, Hawaii, Idaho, Illinois, Indiana, Maine, Minnesota, Mississippi, Montana, Nebraska, Nevada, New Mexico, New York, North Dakota, Oregon, South Carolina, South Dakota, Tennessee, Utah, Washington, West Virginia.

18 Delaware, Georgia, Iowa, Kansas, Kentucky, Massachusetts, Missouri, New Jersey, North Carolina, Oklahoma, Pennsylvania, Rhode Island, Virginia, Wyoming.

19 Louisiana

20 New Hampshire

21 Texas

* For an explanation of survivors/descendants, see page 32.
** For an explanation of families/persons, see page 33.
*** For an explanation of children's guardians and trust, see page 35.

Asset and Beneficiary List

Property Inventory

Assets

Bank Accounts (checking, savings, certificates of deposit)

_____
_____
_____
_____
_____
_____
_____
_____

Real Estate

_____
_____
_____
_____
_____
_____
_____
_____

Vehicles (cars, trucks, boats, planes, RVs, etc.)

_____
_____
_____
_____
_____
_____
_____
_____

Personal Property (collections, jewelry, tools, artwork, household items, etc.)

_____
_____
_____
_____
_____
_____
_____
_____

_____

_____

_____

_____

_____

_____

_____

Stocks/Bonds/Mutual Funds

_____

_____

_____

_____

_____

_____

_____

_____

_____

_____

_____

_____

_____

Retirement Accounts (IRAs, 401(k)s, pension plans, etc.)

_____

_____

_____

_____

_____

_____

Receivables (mortgages held, notes, accounts receivable, personal loans)

_____

_____

_____

_____

_____

Life Insurance

_____
_____
_____
_____
_____
_____
_____

Other Property (trusts, partnerships, businesses, profit sharing, copyrights, etc.)

_____
_____
_____
_____
_____
_____
_____

Liabilities

Real Estate Loans

_____
_____
_____
_____
_____
_____
_____

Vehicle Loans

_____
_____
_____
_____
_____
_____
_____

Other Secured Loans

_____
_____
_____
_____
_____
_____
_____

Unsecured Loans and Debts (taxes, child support, judgments, etc.)

_____
_____
_____
_____
_____
_____
_____

Beneficiary List

Name_____ Address_____ Phone_____

_____
_____
_____
_____
_____
_____
_____

Preferences and Information List
STATEMENT OF DESIRES AND LOCATION OF PROPERTY & DOCUMENTS

I, _____, am signing this document as the expression of my desires as to the matters stated below, and to inform my family members or other significant persons of the location of certain property and documents in the event of any emergency or of my death.

1. **Funeral Desires.** It is my desire that the following arrangements be made for my funeral and disposition of remains in the event of my death (state if you have made any arrangements, such as pre-paid burial plans, cemetery plots owned, etc.):

   o   Burial at _____
   _____.

   o   Cremation at _____
   _____.

   o   Other specific desires: _____
   _____
   _____.

2. **Pets.** I have the following pet(s): _____
   _____. The following are my desires concerning the care of said pet(s): _____
   _____
   _____.

4. **Notification.** I would like the following person(s) notified in the event of emergency or death (give name, address and phone number):

   _____
   _____
   _____
   _____
   _____.

5. **Location of Documents.** The following is a list of important documents, and their location:

   o   Last Will and Testament, dated _____. Location: _____
   _____.

   o   Durable Power of Attorney, dated _____. Location: _____
   _____.

   o   Living Will, dated _____. Location: _____
   _____.

   o   Deed(s) to real estate (describe property location and location of deed):
   _____
   _____
   _____

- Title(s) to vehicles (cars, boats, etc.) (Describe vehicle, its location, and location of title, registration, or other documents):

  _____
  _____
  _____
  _____

- Life insurance policies (list name address & phone number of insurance company and insurance agent, policy number, and location of policy):

  _____
  _____
  _____

- Other insurance policies (list type, company & agent, policy number, and location of policy):

  _____
  _____
  _____

- Other: (list other documents such as stock certificates, bonds, certificates of deposit, etc., and their location):

  _____
  _____
  _____

6. **Location of Assets.** In addition to items readily visible in my home or listed above, I have the following assets:

   - Safe deposit box located at _____, box number _____. Key located at: _____.

   - Bank accounts (list name & address of bank, type of account, and account number):

     _____

   - Other (describe the item and give its location):

     _____
     _____
     _____
     _____
     _____

7. Other desires or information (state any desires or provide any information not given above; use additional sheets of paper if necessary):

   _____
   _____
   _____
   _____
   _____

Dated: _____

_____
Signature

Last Will and Testament

I, _____ a resident of _____
County, _____ do hereby make, publish, and declare this to be my Last Will
and Testament, hereby revoking any and all Wills and Codicils heretofore made by me.

    FIRST: I direct that all my just debts and funeral expenses be paid out of my estate as soon
after my death as is practicable.

    SECOND: I give, devise, and bequeath the following specific gifts:

_____

_____

_____

_____

_____

_____

_____

_____

_____

_____

    THIRD: I give, devise, and bequeath all my estate, real, personal, and mixed, of whatever
kind and wherever situated, of which I may die seized or possessed, or in which I may have any
interest or over which I may have any power of appointment or testamentary disposition, to my
spouse, _____. If my said spouse does not survive me,
I give, and bequeath the said property to my children _____

_____

_____,
plus any afterborn or adopted children in equal shares or their lineal descendants, per stirpes.

    FOURTH: In the event that any beneficiary fails to survive me by thirty days, then this will
shall take effect as if that person had predeceased me.

    FIFTH: Should my spouse not survive me, I hereby nominate, constitute, and appoint
_____ as guardian over the person and estate of any of
my children who have not reached the age of majority at the time of my death. In the event that said
guardian is unable or unwilling to serve, then I nominate, constitute, and appoint
_____ as guardian. Said guardian shall serve without bond
or surety.

    SIXTH: I hereby nominate, constitute, and appoint _____
as Executor or Personal Representative of this, my Last Will and Testament. In the event that such
named person is unable or unwilling to serve at any time or for any reason, then I nominate,
constitute, and appoint _____ as Executor or Personal

Representative in the place and stead of the person first named herein. It is my will and I direct that my Executor or Personal Representative shall not be required to furnish a bond for the faithful performance of his or her duties in any jurisdiction, any provision of law to the contrary notwithstanding, and I give my Executor or Personal Representative full power to administer my estate, including the power to settle claims, pay debts, and sell, lease or exchange real and personal property without court order.

IN WITNESS WHEREOF I declare this to be my Last Will and Testament and execute it willingly as my free and voluntary act for the purposes expressed herein and I am of legal age and sound mind and make this under no constraint or undue influence, this _____ day of _____, 20___ at _____ State of _____.

_____

The foregoing instrument was on said date subscribed at the end thereof by _____, the above named Testator who signed, published, and declared this instrument to be his/her Last Will and Testament in the presence of us and each of us, who thereupon at his/her request, in his/her presence, and in the presence of each other, have hereunto subscribed our names as witnesses thereto. We are of sound mind and proper age to witness a will and understand this to be his/her will, and to the best of our knowledge testator is of legal age to make a will, of sound mind, and under no constraint or undue influence.

_____residing at_____

_____residing at_____

_____residing at_____

Last Will and Testament

I, _____ a resident of _____
County, _____ do hereby make, publish, and declare this to be my Last Will
and Testament, hereby revoking any and all Wills and Codicils heretofore made by me.

FIRST: I direct that all my just debts and funeral expenses be paid out of my estate as soon
after my death as is practicable.

SECOND: I give, devise, and bequeath the following specific gifts:

_____
_____
_____
_____
_____
_____
_____
_____
_____
_____

THIRD: I give, devise, and bequeath all my estate, real, personal, and mixed, of whatever
kind and wherever situated, of which I may die seized or possessed, or in which I may have any
interest or over which I may have any power of appointment or testamentary disposition, to my
spouse, _____. If my said spouse does not survive me,
I give, and bequeath the said property to my children _____
_____
_____,
plus any afterborn or adopted children in equal shares or their lineal descendants, per stirpes.

FOURTH: In the event that any beneficiary fails to survive me by thirty days, then this will
shall take effect as if that person had predeceased me.

FIFTH: Should my spouse not survive me, I hereby nominate, constitute, and appoint
_____, as guardian over the person of any of my children who
have not reached the age of majority at the time of my death. In the event that said guardian is unable
or unwilling to serve, then I nominate, constitute, and appoint _____
as guardian. Said guardian shall serve without bond or surety.

SIXTH: Should my spouse not survive me, I hereby nominate, constitute, and appoint
_____ as guardian over the estate of any of my children who have
not reached the age of majority at the time of my death. In the event that said guardian is unable or
unwilling to serve, then I nominate, constitute, and appoint _____
as guardian. Said guardian shall serve without bond or surety.

Initials: _____ _____ _____ _____ Page ____ of ____ **85**
           Testator   Witness   Witness   Witness

SEVENTH: I hereby nominate, constitute, and appoint _____
as Executor or Personal Representative of this, my Last Will and Testament. In the event that such named person is unable or unwilling to serve at any time or for any reason, then I nominate, constitute, and appoint _____ as Executor or Personal Representative in the place and stead of the person first named herein. It is my will and I direct that my Executor or Personal Representative shall not be required to furnish a bond for the faithful performance of his or her duties in any jurisdiction, any provision of law to the contrary notwithstanding, and I give my Executor or Personal Representative full power to administer my estate, including the power to settle claims, pay debts, and sell, lease or exchange real and personal property without court order.

IN WITNESS WHEREOF I declare this to be my Last Will and Testament and execute it willingly as my free and voluntary act for the purposes expressed herein and I am of legal age and sound mind and make this under no constraint or undue influence, this _____ day of _____, 20___ at _____ State of _____.

_____

The foregoing instrument was on said date subscribed at the end thereof by _____, the above named Testator who signed, published, and declared this instrument to be his/her Last Will and Testament in the presence of us and each of us, who thereupon at his/her request, in his/her presence, and in the presence of each other, have hereunto subscribed our names as witnesses thereto. We are of sound mind and proper age to witness a will and understand this to be his/her will, and to the best of our knowledge testator is of legal age to make a will, of sound mind, and under no constraint or undue influence.

_____residing at_____

_____residing at_____

_____residing at_____

Last Will and Testament

I, _____ a resident of _____
County, _____ do hereby make, publish, and declare this to be my Last Will
and Testament, hereby revoking any and all Wills and Codicils heretofore made by me.

     FIRST: I direct that all my just debts and funeral expenses be paid out of my estate as soon
after my death as is practicable.

     SECOND: I give, devise, and bequeath the following specific gifts:

_____
_____
_____
_____
_____
_____
_____
_____
_____
_____
_____

     THIRD: I give, devise, and bequeath all my estate, real, personal, and mixed, of whatever
kind and wherever situated, of which I may die seized or possessed, or in which I may have any
interest or over which I may have any power of appointment or testamentary disposition, to my
spouse, _____. If my said spouse does not survive me,
I give, and bequeath the said property to my children _____
_____
_____,
plus any afterborn or adopted children in equal shares or their lineal descendants, per stirpes.

     FOURTH: In the event that any beneficiary fails to survive me by thirty days, then this will
shall take effect as if that person had predeceased me.

     FIFTH: In the event that any of my children have not reached the age of _____ years at
the time of my death, then the share of any such child shall be held in a separate trust by
_____ for such child.

The trustee shall use the income and that part of the principal of the trust as is, in the trustee's sole
discretion, necessary or desirable to provide proper housing, medical care, food, clothing, entertainment and education for the trust beneficiary, considering the beneficiary's other resources. Any
income that is not distributed shall be added to the principal. Additionally, the trustee shall have all
powers conferred by the law of the state having jurisdiction over this trust, as well as the power to
pay from the assets of the trust reasonable fees necessary to administer the trust.

The trust shall terminate when the child reaches the age specified above and the remaining assets
distributed to the child, unless they have been exhausted sooner. In the event the child dies prior to

the termination of the trust, then the assets shall pass to the estate of the child. The interests of the beneficiary under this trust shall not be assignable and shall be free from the claims of creditors to the full extent allowed by law.

In the event the said trustee is unable or unwilling to serve for any reason, then I nominate, constitute, and appoint _____as alternate trustee. No bond shall be required of either trustee in any jurisdiction and this trust shall be administered without court supervision as allowed by law.

SIXTH: Should my spouse not survive me, I hereby nominate, constitute, and appoint_____as guardian over the person and estate of any of my children who have not reached the age of majority at the time of my death. In the event that said guardian is unable or unwilling to serve, then I nominate, constitute, and appoint_____ as guardian.

SEVENTH: I hereby nominate, constitute, and appoint _____ as Executor or Personal Representative of this, my Last Will and Testament. In the event that such named person is unable or unwilling to serve at any time or for any reason, then I nominate, constitute, and appoint _____ as Executor or Personal Representative in the place and stead of the person first named herein. It is my will and I direct that my Executor or Personal Representative shall not be required to furnish a bond for the faithful performance of his or her duties in any jurisdiction, any provision of law to the contrary notwithstanding, and I give my Executor or Personal Representative full power to administer my estate, including the power to settle claims, pay debts, and sell, lease or exchange real and personal property without court order.

IN WITNESS WHEREOF I declare this to be my Last Will and Testament and execute it willingly as my free and voluntary act for the purposes expressed herein and I am of legal age and sound mind and make this under no constraint or undue influence, this _____ day of _____, 20___ at _____ State of _____.

_____

The foregoing instrument was on said date subscribed at the end thereof by _____, the above named Testator who signed, published, and declared this instrument to be his/her Last Will and Testament in the presence of us and each of us, who thereupon at his/her request, in his/her presence, and in the presence of each other, have hereunto subscribed our names as witnesses thereto. We are of sound mind and proper age to witness a will and understand this to be his/her will, and to the best of our knowledge testator is of legal age to make a will, of sound mind, and under no constraint or undue influence.

_____residing at_____

_____residing at_____

_____residing at_____

Last Will and Testament

I, _____ a resident of _____
County, _____ do hereby make, publish, and declare this to be my Last Will
and Testament, hereby revoking any and all Wills and Codicils heretofore made by me.

FIRST: I direct that all my just debts and funeral expenses be paid out of my estate as soon
after my death as is practicable.

SECOND: I give, devise, and bequeath the following specific gifts:

_____

_____

_____

_____

_____

_____

_____

_____

_____

_____

THIRD: I give, devise, and bequeath all my estate, real, personal, and mixed, of whatever
kind and wherever situated, of which I may die seized or possessed, or in which I may have any
interest or over which I may have any power of appointment or testamentary disposition, to my
spouse, _____. If my said spouse does not survive me,
I give, and bequeath the said property to _____

_____

_____,
or the survivor of them.

FOURTH: In the event that any beneficiary fails to survive me by thirty days, then this will
shall take effect as if that person had predeceased me.

FIFTH: I hereby nominate, constitute, and appoint _____
as Executor or Personal Representative of this, my Last Will and Testament. In the event that such
named person is unable or unwilling to serve at any time or for any reason, then I nominate,
constitute, and appoint _____ as Executor or Personal
Representative in the place and stead of the person first named herein. It is my will and I direct that
my Executor or Personal Representative shall not be required to furnish a bond for the faithful
performance of his or her duties in any jurisdiction, any provision of law to the contrary
notwithstanding, and I give my Executor or Personal Representative full power to administer my
estate, including the power to settle claims, pay debts, and sell, lease or exchange real and personal
property without court order.

IN WITNESS WHEREOF I declare this to be my Last Will and Testament and execute it willingly as my free and voluntary act for the purposes expressed herein and I am of legal age and sound mind and make this under no constraint or undue influence, this _____ day of _____, 20___ at _____ State of _____.

_____

The foregoing instrument was on said date subscribed at the end thereof by _____, the above named Testator who signed, published, and declared this instrument to be his/her Last Will and Testament in the presence of us and each of us, who thereupon at his/her request, in his/her presence, and in the presence of each other, have hereunto subscribed our names as witnesses thereto. We are of sound mind and proper age to witness a will and understand this to be his/her will, and to the best of our knowledge testator is of legal age to make a will, of sound mind, and under no constraint or undue influence.

_____residing at_____

_____residing at_____

_____residing at_____

Last Will and Testament

I, _____ a resident of _____ County, _____ do hereby make, publish, and declare this to be my Last Will and Testament, hereby revoking any and all Wills and Codicils heretofore made by me.

FIRST: I direct that all my just debts and funeral expenses be paid out of my estate as soon after my death as is practicable.

SECOND: I give, devise, and bequeath the following specific gifts:

_____

_____

_____

_____

_____

_____

_____

_____

_____

_____

THIRD: I give, devise, and bequeath all my estate, real, personal, and mixed, of whatever kind and wherever situated, of which I may die seized or possessed, or in which I may have any interest or over which I may have any power of appointment or testamentary disposition, to my spouse, _____. If my said spouse does not survive me, I give, and bequeath the said property to _____ _____ _____, or to their lineal descendants, per stirpes.

FOURTH: In the event that any beneficiary fails to survive me by thirty days, then this will shall take effect as if that person had predeceased me.

FIFTH: I hereby nominate, constitute, and appoint _____ as Executor or Personal Representative of this, my Last Will and Testament. In the event that such named person is unable or unwilling to serve at any time or for any reason, then I nominate, constitute, and appoint _____ as Executor or Personal Representative in the place and stead of the person first named herein. It is my will and I direct that my Executor or Personal Representative shall not be required to furnish a bond for the faithful performance of his or her duties in any jurisdiction, any provision of law to the contrary notwithstanding, and I give my Executor or Personal Representative full power to administer my estate, including the power to settle claims, pay debts, and sell, lease or exchange real and personal property without court order.

IN WITNESS WHEREOF I declare this to be my Last Will and Testament and execute it willingly as my free and voluntary act for the purposes expressed herein and I am of legal age and sound mind and make this under no constraint or undue influence, this _____ day of _____, 20___ at _____ State of _____.

_____

The foregoing instrument was on said date subscribed at the end thereof by _____, the above named Testator who signed, published, and declared this instrument to be his/her Last Will and Testament in the presence of us and each of us, who thereupon at his/her request, in his/her presence, and in the presence of each other, have hereunto subscribed our names as witnesses thereto. We are of sound mind and proper age to witness a will and understand this to be his/her will, and to the best of our knowledge testator is of legal age to make a will, of sound mind, and under no constraint or undue influence.

_____residing at_____

_____residing at_____

_____residing at_____

Last Will and Testament

I, _____ a resident of _____
County, _____ do hereby make, publish, and declare this to be my Last Will
and Testament, hereby revoking any and all Wills and Codicils heretofore made by me.

FIRST: I direct that all my just debts and funeral expenses be paid out of my estate as soon
after my death as is practicable.

SECOND: I give, devise, and bequeath the following specific gifts:

_____
_____
_____
_____
_____
_____
_____
_____
_____
_____

THIRD: I give, devise, and bequeath all my estate, real, personal, and mixed, of whatever
kind and wherever situated, of which I may die seized or possessed, or in which I may have any
interest or over which I may have any power of appointment or testamentary disposition, to my
spouse, _____. If my said spouse does not survive me,
I give, and bequeath the said property to my children _____
_____
_____,
in equal shares or to their lineal descendants, per stirpes.

FOURTH: In the event that any beneficiary fails to survive me by thirty days, then this will
shall take effect as if that person had predeceased me.

FIFTH: I hereby nominate, constitute, and appoint _____ as
Executor or Personal Representative of this, my Last Will and Testament. In the event that such
named person is unable or unwilling to serve at any time or for any reason, then I nominate,
constitute, and appoint _____ as Executor or Personal
Representative in the place and stead of the person first named herein. It is my will and I direct that
my Executor or Personal Representative shall not be required to furnish a bond for the faithful
performance of his or her duties in any jurisdiction, any provision of law to the contrary
notwithstanding, and I give my Executor or Personal Representative full power to administer my
estate, including the power to settle claims, pay debts, and sell, lease or exchange real and personal
property without court order.

IN WITNESS WHEREOF I declare this to be my Last Will and Testament and execute it willingly as my free and voluntary act for the purposes expressed herein and I am of legal age and sound mind and make this under no constraint or undue influence, this _____ day of _____, 20____ at _____ State of _____.

_____

The foregoing instrument was on said date subscribed at the end thereof by _____, the above named Testator who signed, published, and declared this instrument to be his/her Last Will and Testament in the presence of us and each of us, who thereupon at his/her request, in his/her presence, and in the presence of each other, have hereunto subscribed our names as witnesses thereto. We are of sound mind and proper age to witness a will and understand this to be his/her will, and to the best of our knowledge testator is of legal age to make a will, of sound mind, and under no constraint or undue influence.

_____residing at_____

_____residing at_____

_____residing at_____

Last Will and Testament

I, _____ a resident of _____
County, _____ do hereby make, publish, and declare this to be my Last Will
and Testament, hereby revoking any and all Wills and Codicils heretofore made by me.

FIRST: I direct that all my just debts and funeral expenses be paid out of my estate as soon
after my death as is practicable.

SECOND: I give, devise, and bequeath the following specific gifts:

_____

_____

_____

_____

_____

_____

_____

_____

_____

_____

THIRD: I give, devise, and bequeath all my estate, real, personal, and mixed, of whatever
kind and wherever situated, of which I may die seized or possessed, or in which I may have any
interest or over which I may have any power of appointment or testamentary disposition, as follows:
_____% to my spouse, _____ and
_____% to my children, _____

_____

_____,
in equal shares or to their lineal descendants per stirpes.

FOURTH: In the event that any beneficiary fails to survive me by thirty days, then this will
shall take effect as if that person had predeceased me.

SIXTH: I hereby nominate, constitute, and appoint _____ as
Executor or Personal Representative of this, my Last Will and Testament. In the event that such named
person is unable or unwilling to serve at any time or for any reason, then I nominate, constitute, and
appoint _____ as Executor or Personal Representative in the place
and stead of the person first named herein. It is my will and I direct that my Executor or Personal
Representative shall not be required to furnish a bond for the faithful performance of his or her
duties in any jurisdiction, any provision of law to the contrary notwithstanding, and I give my
Executor or Personal Representative full power to administer my estate, including the power to
settle claims, pay debts, and sell, lease or exchange real and personal property without court order.

IN WITNESS WHEREOF I declare this to be my Last Will and Testament and execute it willingly as my free and voluntary act for the purposes expressed herein and I am of legal age and sound mind and make this under no constraint or undue influence, this _____ day of _____, 20___ at _____ State of _____.

_____

The foregoing instrument was on said date subscribed at the end thereof by _____, the above named Testator who signed, published, and declared this instrument to be his/her Last Will and Testament in the presence of us and each of us, who thereupon at his/her request, in his/her presence, and in the presence of each other, have hereunto subscribed our names as witnesses thereto. We are of sound mind and proper age to witness a will and understand this to be his/her will, and to the best of our knowledge testator is of legal age to make a will, of sound mind, and under no constraint or undue influence.

_____residing at_____

_____residing at_____

_____residing at_____

Last Will and Testament

I, _____ a resident of _____ County, _____ do hereby make, publish, and declare this to be my Last Will and Testament, hereby revoking any and all Wills and Codicils heretofore made by me.

FIRST: I direct that all my just debts and funeral expenses be paid out of my estate as soon after my death as is practicable.

SECOND: I give, devise, and bequeath the following specific gifts:

_____

_____

_____

_____

_____

_____

_____

_____

_____

_____

THIRD: I give, devise, and bequeath all my estate, real, personal, and mixed, of whatever kind and wherever situated, of which I may die seized or possessed, or in which I may have any interest or over which I may have any power of appointment or testamentary disposition, to my children _____

_____

_____,

plus any afterborn or adopted children in equal shares or to their lineal descendants per stirpes.

FOURTH: In the event that any beneficiary fails to survive me by thirty days, then this will shall take effect as if that person had predeceased me.

FIFTH: In the event any of my children have not attained the age of 18 years at the time of my death, I hereby nominate, constitute, and appoint _____ as guardian over the person and estate of any of my children who have not reached the age of majority at the time of my death. In the event that said guardian is unable or unwilling to serve, then I nominate, constitute, and appoint _____ as guardian. Said guardian shall serve without bond or surety.

SIXTH: I hereby nominate, constitute, and appoint _____ as Executor or Personal Representative of this, my Last Will and Testament. In the event that such named person is unable or unwilling to serve at any time or for any reason, then I nominate, constitute, and appoint _____ as Executor or Personal Representative in the place and stead of the person first named herein. It is my will and I direct that my Executor or Personal

Representative shall not be required to furnish a bond for the faithful performance of his or her duties in any jurisdiction, any provision of law to the contrary notwithstanding, and I give my Executor or Personal Representative full power to administer my estate, including the power to settle claims, pay debts, and sell, lease or exchange real and personal property without court order.

IN WITNESS WHEREOF I declare this to be my Last Will and Testament and execute it willingly as my free and voluntary act for the purposes expressed herein and I am of legal age and sound mind and make this under no constraint or undue influence, this _____ day of _____, 20___ at _____ State of _____.

_____

The foregoing instrument was on said date subscribed at the end thereof by _____, the above named Testator who signed, published, and declared this instrument to be his/her Last Will and Testament in the presence of us and each of us, who thereupon at his/her request, in his/her presence, and in the presence of each other, have hereunto subscribed our names as witnesses thereto. We are of sound mind and proper age to witness a will and understand this to be his/her will, and to the best of our knowledge testator is of legal age to make a will, of sound mind, and under no constraint or undue influence.

_____residing at_____

_____residing at_____

_____residing at_____

Last Will and Testament

I, _____ a resident of _____
County, _____ do hereby make, publish, and declare this to be my Last Will and Testament, hereby revoking any and all Wills and Codicils heretofore made by me.

FIRST: I direct that all my just debts and funeral expenses be paid out of my estate as soon after my death as is practicable.

SECOND: I give, devise, and bequeath the following specific gifts:

_____

_____

_____

_____

_____

_____

_____

_____

_____

_____

THIRD: I give, devise, and bequeath all my estate, real, personal, and mixed, of whatever kind and wherever situated, of which I may die seized or possessed, or in which I may have any interest or over which I may have any power of appointment or testamentary disposition, to my children

_____

_____

_____,

plus any afterborn or adopted children in equal shares or to their lineal descendants per stirpes.

FOURTH: In the event that any beneficiary fails to survive me by thirty days, then this will shall take effect as if that person had predeceased me.

FIFTH: In the event any of my children have not attained the age of 18 years at the time of my death, I hereby nominate, constitute, and appoint _____
as guardian over the person of any of my children who have not reached the age of majority at the time of my death. In the event that said guardian is unable or unwilling to serve, then I nominate, constitute, and appoint _____ as guardian. Said guardian shall serve without bond or surety.

SIXTH: In the event any of my children have not attained the age of 18 years at the time of my death, I hereby nominate, constitute, and appoint _____
as guardian over the estate of any of my children who have not reached the age of majority at the time of my death. In the event that said guardian is unable or unwilling to serve, then I nominate, constitute, and appoint _____ as guardian. Said guardian shall serve without bond or surety.

Initials: _____ _____ _____ _____   Page ____ of ____   **99**
       Testator   Witness   Witness   Witness

SEVENTH: I hereby nominate, constitute, and appoint _____ as Executor or Personal Representative of this, my Last Will and Testament. In the event that such named person is unable or unwilling to serve at any time or for any reason, then I nominate, constitute, and appoint _____ as Executor or Personal Representative in the place and stead of the person first named herein. It is my will and I direct that my Executor or Personal Representative shall not be required to furnish a bond for the faithful performance of his or her duties in any jurisdiction, any provision of law to the contrary notwithstanding, and I give my Executor or Personal Representative full power to administer my estate, including the power to settle claims, pay debts, and sell, lease or exchange real and personal property without court order.

IN WITNESS WHEREOF I declare this to be my Last Will and Testament and execute it willingly as my free and voluntary act for the purposes expressed herein and I am of legal age and sound mind and make this under no constraint or undue influence, this _____ day of _____, 20___ at _____ State of _____.

_____

The foregoing instrument was on said date subscribed at the end thereof by _____, the above named Testator who signed, published, and declared this instrument to be his/her Last Will and Testament in the presence of us and each of us, who thereupon at his/her request, in his/her presence, and in the presence of each other, have hereunto subscribed our names as witnesses thereto. We are of sound mind and proper age to witness a will and understand this to be his/her will, and to the best of our knowledge testator is of legal age to make a will, of sound mind, and under no constraint or undue influence.

_____residing at_____

_____residing at_____

_____residing at_____

Last Will and Testament

I, _____ a resident of _____ County, _____ do hereby make, publish, and declare this to be my Last Will and Testament, hereby revoking any and all Wills and Codicils heretofore made by me.

FIRST: I direct that all my just debts and funeral expenses be paid out of my estate as soon after my death as is practicable.

SECOND: I give, devise, and bequeath the following specific gifts:

_____

_____

_____

_____

_____

_____

_____

_____

_____

THIRD: I give, devise, and bequeath all my estate, real, personal, and mixed, of whatever kind and wherever situated, of which I may die seized or possessed, or in which I may have any interest or over which I may have any power of appointment or testamentary disposition, to my children

_____

_____

_____,

plus any afterborn or adopted children in equal shares or to their lineal descendants per stirpes.

FOURTH: In the event that any beneficiary fails to survive me by thirty days, then this will shall take effect as if that person had predeceased me.

FIFTH: In the event that any of my children have not reached the age of _____ years at the time of my death, then the share of any such child shall be held in a separate trust by _____ for such child.

The trustee shall use the income and that part of the principal of the trust as is, in the trustee's sole discretion, necessary or desirable to provide proper housing, medical care, food, clothing, entertainment and education for the trust beneficiary, considering the beneficiary's other resources. Any income that is not distributed shall be added to the principal. Additionally, the trustee shall have all powers conferred by the law of the state having jurisdiction over this trust, as well as the power to pay from the assets of the trust reasonable fees necessary to administer the trust.

The trust shall terminate when the child reaches the age specified above and the remaining assets distributed to the child, unless they have been exhausted sooner. In the event the child dies prior to the termination of the trust, then the assets shall pass to the estate of the child. The interests of the

Initials: _____ _____ _____ _____   Page ____ of ____   **101**
     Testator   Witness   Witness   Witness

beneficiary under this trust shall not be assignable and shall be free from the claims of creditors to the full extent allowed by law.

In the event the said trustee is unable or unwilling to serve for any reason, then I nominate, constitute, and appoint _____as alternate trustee. No bond shall be required of either trustee in any jurisdiction and this trust shall be administered without court supervision as allowed by law.

SIXTH: In the event any of my children have not attained the age of 18 years at the time of my death, I hereby nominate, constitute, and appoint _____as guardian over the person and estate of any of my children who have not reached the age of majority at the time of my death. In the event that said guardian is unable or unwilling to serve, then I nominate, constitute, and appoint _____ as guardian. Said guardian shall serve without bond or surety.

SEVENTH: I hereby nominate, constitute, and appoint _____ as Executor or Personal Representative of this, my Last Will and Testament. In the event that such named person is unable or unwilling to serve at any time or for any reason, then I nominate, constitute, and appoint _____ as Executor or Personal Representative in the place and stead of the person first named herein. It is my will and I direct that my Executor or Personal Representative shall not be required to furnish a bond for the faithful performance of his or her duties in any jurisdiction, any provision of law to the contrary notwithstanding, and I give my Executor or Personal Representative full power to administer my estate, including the power to settle claims, pay debts, and sell, lease or exchange real and personal property without court order.

IN WITNESS WHEREOF I declare this to be my Last Will and Testament and execute it willingly as my free and voluntary act for the purposes expressed herein and I am of legal age and sound mind and make this under no constraint or undue influence, this _____ day of _____, _____ at _____ State of _____.

_____

The foregoing instrument was on said date subscribed at the end thereof by _____, the above named Testator who signed, published, and declared this instrument to be his/her Last Will and Testament in the presence of us and each of us, who thereupon at his/her request, in his/her presence, and in the presence of each other, have hereunto subscribed our names as witnesses thereto. We are of sound mind and proper age to witness a will and understand this to be his/her will, and to the best of our knowledge testator is of legal age to make a will, of sound mind, and under no constraint or undue influence.

_____residing at_____

_____residing at_____

_____residing at_____

Last Will and Testament

I, _____ a resident of _____ County, _____ do hereby make, publish, and declare this to be my Last Will and Testament, hereby revoking any and all Wills and Codicils heretofore made by me.

FIRST: I direct that all my just debts and funeral expenses be paid out of my estate as soon after my death as is practicable.

SECOND: I give, devise, and bequeath the following specific gifts:

_____

_____

_____

_____

_____

_____

_____

_____

_____

_____

_____

THIRD: I give, devise, and bequeath all my estate, real, personal, and mixed, of whatever kind and wherever situated, of which I may die seized or possessed, or in which I may have any interest or over which I may have any power of appointment or testamentary disposition, to my children _____

_____

_____,

in equal shares, or their lineal descendants per stirpes.

FOURTH: In the event that any beneficiary fails to survive me by thirty days, then this will shall take effect as if that person had predeceased me.

FIFTH: I hereby nominate, constitute, and appoint _____ as Executor or Personal Representative of this, my Last Will and Testament. In the event that such named person is unable or unwilling to serve at any time or for any reason, then I nominate, constitute, and appoint _____ as Executor or Personal Representative in the place and stead of the person first named herein. It is my will and I direct that my Executor or Personal Representative shall not be required to furnish a bond for the faithful performance of his or her duties in any jurisdiction, any provision of law to the contrary notwithstanding, and I give my Executor or Personal Representative full power to administer my estate, including the power to settle claims, pay debts, and sell, lease or exchange real and personal property without court order.

Initials: _____ _____ _____ _____   Page ____ of ____   **103**
Testator   Witness   Witness   Witness

IN WITNESS WHEREOF I declare this to be my Last Will and Testament and execute it willingly as my free and voluntary act for the purposes expressed herein and I am of legal age and sound mind and make this under no constraint or undue influence, this _____ day of _____, 20___ at _____ State of _____.

_____

The foregoing instrument was on said date subscribed at the end thereof by _____, the above named Testator who signed, published, and declared this instrument to be his/her Last Will and Testament in the presence of us and each of us, who thereupon at his/her request, in his/her presence, and in the presence of each other, have hereunto subscribed our names as witnesses thereto. We are of sound mind and proper age to witness a will and understand this to be his/her will, and to the best of our knowledge testator is of legal age to make a will, of sound mind, and under no constraint or undue influence.

_____residing at_____

_____residing at_____

_____residing at_____

Last Will and Testament

I, _____ a resident of _____ County, _____ do hereby make, publish, and declare this to be my Last Will and Testament, hereby revoking any and all Wills and Codicils heretofore made by me.

FIRST: I direct that all my just debts and funeral expenses be paid out of my estate as soon after my death as is practicable.

SECOND: I give, devise, and bequeath the following specific gifts:

_____

_____

_____

_____

_____

_____

_____

_____

_____

_____

THIRD: I give, devise, and bequeath all my estate, real, personal, and mixed, of whatever kind and wherever situated, of which I may die seized or possessed, or in which I may have any interest or over which I may have any power of appointment or testamentary disposition, to my children _____

_____

_____,

in equal shares, or their lineal descendants per capita.

FOURTH: In the event that any beneficiary fails to survive me by thirty days, then this will shall take effect as if that person had predeceased me.

FIFTH: I hereby nominate, constitute, and appoint _____ as Executor or Personal Representative of this, my Last Will and Testament. In the event that such named person is unable or unwilling to serve at any time or for any reason, then I nominate, constitute, and appoint _____ as Executor or Personal Representative in the place and stead of the person first named herein. It is my will and I direct that my Executor or Personal Representative shall not be required to furnish a bond for the faithful performance of his or her duties in any jurisdiction, any provision of law to the contrary notwithstanding, and I give my Executor or Personal Representative full power to administer my estate, including the power to settle claims, pay debts, and sell, lease or exchange real and personal property without court order.

IN WITNESS WHEREOF I declare this to be my Last Will and Testament and execute it willingly as my free and voluntary act for the purposes expressed herein and I am of legal age and

Initials: _____ _____ _____ _____   Page ____ of ____   **105**
       Testator   Witness   Witness   Witness

sound mind and make this under no constraint or undue influence, this _____ day of
_____, 20___ at _____ State of _____.

_____

The foregoing instrument was on said date subscribed at the end thereof by
_____, the above named Testator who signed, published, and declared this instrument to be his/her Last Will and Testament in the presence of us and each of us, who thereupon at his/her request, in his/her presence, and in the presence of each other, have hereunto subscribed our names as witnesses thereto. We are of sound mind and proper age to witness a will and understand this to be his/her will, and to the best of our knowledge testator is of legal age to make a will, of sound mind, and under no constraint or undue influence.

_____residing at_____

_____residing at_____

_____residing at_____

Last Will and Testament

I, _____ a resident of _____ County, _____ do hereby make, publish, and declare this to be my Last Will and Testament, hereby revoking any and all Wills and Codicils heretofore made by me.

FIRST: I direct that all my just debts and funeral expenses be paid out of my estate as soon after my death as is practicable.

SECOND: I give, devise, and bequeath the following specific gifts:

_____
_____
_____
_____
_____
_____
_____
_____
_____
_____
_____

THIRD: I give, devise, and bequeath all my estate, real, personal, and mixed, of whatever kind and wherever situated, of which I may die seized or possessed, or in which I may have any interest or over which I may have any power of appointment or testamentary disposition, to the following:

_____
_____
_____,
in equal share, or to the survivor of them.

FOURTH: In the event that any beneficiary fails to survive me by thirty days, then this will shall take effect as if that person had predeceased me.

FIFTH: I hereby nominate, constitute, and appoint _____ as Executor or Personal Representative of this, my Last Will and Testament. In the event that such named person is unable or unwilling to serve at any time or for any reason, then I nominate, constitute, and appoint _____ as Executor or Personal Representative in the place and stead of the person first named herein. It is my will and I direct that my Executor or Personal Representative shall not be required to furnish a bond for the faithful performance of his or her duties in any jurisdiction, any provision of law to the contrary notwithstanding, and I give my Executor or Personal Representative full power to administer my estate, including the power to settle claims, pay debts, and sell, lease or exchange real and personal property without court order.

IN WITNESS WHEREOF I declare this to be my Last Will and Testament and execute it willingly as my free and voluntary act for the purposes expressed herein and I am of legal age and

Initials: _____ _____ _____ _____   Page ____ of ____   **107**
     Testator   Witness   Witness   Witness

sound mind and make this under no constraint or undue influence, this _____ day of
_____, 20___ at _____ State of _____.

_____

    The foregoing instrument was on said date subscribed at the end thereof by
_____, the above named Testator who signed, published,
and declared this instrument to be his/her Last Will and Testament in the presence of us and each of
us, who thereupon at his/her request, in his/her presence, and in the presence of each other, have
hereunto subscribed our names as witnesses thereto. We are of sound mind and proper age to witness
a will and understand this to be his/her will, and to the best of our knowledge testator is of legal age
to make a will, of sound mind, and under no constraint or undue influence.

_____residing at_____

_____residing at_____

_____residing at_____

Last Will and Testament

I, _____ a resident of _____
County, _____ do hereby make, publish, and declare this to be my Last Will
and Testament, hereby revoking any and all Wills and Codicils heretofore made by me.

FIRST: I direct that all my just debts and funeral expenses be paid out of my estate as soon
after my death as is practicable.

SECOND: I give, devise, and bequeath the following specific gifts:

_____

_____

_____

_____

_____

_____

_____

_____

_____

_____

THIRD: I give, devise, and bequeath all my estate, real, personal, and mixed, of whatever
kind and wherever situated, of which I may die seized or possessed, or in which I may have any interest
or over which I may have any power of appointment or testamentary disposition, to the following:

_____

_____

_____,

in equal shares, or their lineal descendants per stirpes.

FOURTH: In the event that any beneficiary fails to survive me by thirty days, then this will
shall take effect as if that person had predeceased me.

FIFTH: I hereby nominate, constitute, and appoint _____ as
Executor or Personal Representative of this, my Last Will and Testament. In the event that such named
person is unable or unwilling to serve at any time or for any reason, then I nominate, constitute, and
appoint _____ as Executor or Personal Representative in the place
and stead of the person first named herein. It is my will and I direct that my Executor or Personal
Representative shall not be required to furnish a bond for the faithful performance of his or her
duties in any jurisdiction, any provision of law to the contrary notwithstanding, and I give my
Executor or Personal Representative full power to administer my estate, including the power to
settle claims, pay debts, and sell, lease or exchange real and personal property without court order.

IN WITNESS WHEREOF I declare this to be my Last Will and Testament and execute it
willingly as my free and voluntary act for the purposes expressed herein and I am of legal age and

Initials: _____ _____ _____ _____   Page ____ of ____   **109**
     Testator   Witness   Witness   Witness

sound mind and make this under no constraint or undue influence, this _____ day of _____, 20___ at _____ State of _____.

_____

The foregoing instrument was on said date subscribed at the end thereof by _____, the above named Testator who signed, published, and declared this instrument to be his/her Last Will and Testament in the presence of us and each of us, who thereupon at his/her request, in his/her presence, and in the presence of each other, have hereunto subscribed our names as witnesses thereto. We are of sound mind and proper age to witness a will and understand this to be his/her will, and to the best of our knowledge testator is of legal age to make a will, of sound mind, and under no constraint or undue influence.

_____residing at_____

_____residing at_____

_____residing at_____

Self-Proved Will Affidavit
(attach to Will)

STATE OF _____

COUNTY OF _____

    We, _____, and _____,
and _____, the testator and the witnesses, whose names are signed
to the attached or foregoing instrument in those capacities, personally appearing before the undersigned authority and being first duly sworn, declare to the undersigned authority under penalty of
perjury that: 1) the testator declared, signed, and executed the instrument as his or her last will; 2)
he or she signed it willingly, or directed another to sign for him or her; 3) he or she executed it as
his or her free and voluntary act for the purposes therein expressed; and 4) each of the witnesses,
and the request of the testator, in his or her hearing and presence and in the presence of each other,
signed the will as witnesses, and that to the best of his or her knowledge the testator was at that time
of full legal age, of sound mind, and under no constraint or undue influence.

_____ (Testator)

_____ (Witness)

_____ (Witness)

Subscribed, sworn, and acknowledged before me _____ a
notary public, and by _____, the testator, and by
_____ and _____ ,
witnesses, this _____ day of _____, 20____.

_____
Notary public

Self-Proved Will Affidavit
(attach to Will)

STATE OF _____

COUNTY OF _____

    I, the undersigned, an officer authorized to administer oaths, certify that _____
_____, the testator and
_____, and _____,
the witnesses, whose names are signed to the attached or foregoing instrument and whose signatures
appear below, having appeared before me and having been first been duly sworn, each then declared
to me that: 1) the attached or foregoing instrument is the last will of the testator; 2) the testator
willingly and voluntarily declared, signed, and executed the will in the presence of the witnesses; 3)
the witnesses signed the will upon the request of the testator, in the presence and hearing of the
testator and in the presence of each other; 4) to the best knowledge of each witness, the testator was,
at the time of signing, of the age of majority (or otherwise legally competent to make a will), of
sound mind and memory, and under no constraint or undue influence; and 5) each witness was and
is competent and of proper age to witness a will.

_____ (Testator)

_____ (Witness)

_____ (Witness)

Subscribed and sworn to before me by _____, the testator,
who is personally known to me or who has produced _____
as identification, and by _____, a witness, who
is personally known to me or who has produced _____
as identification, and by _____, a witness, who is
personally known to me or who has produced _____
as identification, this _____ day of_____, 20____.

_____
Notary or other officer

Notarial Will Page—Louisiana
(attach to Will)

STATE OF LOUISIANA

PARRISH OF _____

The testator has signed this will at the end and on each other separate page, and has declared or signified in our presence that it is his/her last will and testament, and in the presence of the testator and each other we have hereunto subscribed our names this _____ day of _____, _____.

_____ (Testator)

_____ (Witness)

_____ (Witness)

On this _____ day of _____, _____ before me personally appeared _____, the testator, and _____, and _____, the witnesses, to me known to be the persons described in and who executed the foregoing instrument, and acknowledged that they executed it as their free act and deed.

Signed:_____
Notary

Note: In Louisiana a will must be signed on all pages by the testator. On page 1 replace "County" with "Parrish."

Self-Proved Will Page—New Hampshire
(attach to Will)

The foregoing instrument was acknowledged before me this _____ (day),

by _____ the testator; _____

and _____, the witnesses, who under oath swear as follows:

    1. The testator signed the instrument as his will or expressly directed another to sign for him.

    2. This was the testator's free and voluntary act for the purposes expressed in the will.

    3. Each witness signed at the request of the testator, in his presence, and in the presence of the other witness.

    4. To the best of my knowledge, at the time of the signing the testator was at least 18 years of age, or if under 18 years was a married person, and was of sane mind and under no constraint or undue influence.

_____
Signature

_____
Official Capacity

Self-Proved Will Affidavit—Texas
(attach to Will)

STATE OF TEXAS

COUNTY OF _____

    Before me, the undersigned authority, on this day personally appeared _____ _____, _____, and _____ _____, known to me to be the testator and the witnesses, respectively, whose names are subscribed to the annexed or foregoing instrument in their respective capacities, and, all of said persons being by me duly sworn, the said _____ _____ testator, declared to me and to the said witnesses in my presence that said instrument is his or her last will and testament, and that he or she had willingly made and executed it as his or her free act and deed, and the said witnesses, each on his or her oath stated to me in the presence and hearing of the said testator, that the said testator had declared to them that said instrument is his or her last will and testament, and that he or she executed same as such and wanted each of them to sign it as a witness; and upon their oaths each witness stated further that they did sign the same as witnesses in the presence of the said testator and at his or her request; that he or she was at the time eighteen years of age or over (or being under such age, was or had been lawfully married, or was then a member of the armed forces of the United States or an auxiliary thereof or of the Maritime Service) and was of sound mind; and that each of said witnesses was then at least fourteen years of age.

_____ (Testator)

_____ (Witness)

_____ (Witness)

Subscribed and sworn to before me by _____, the testator, and by _____, and _____, the witnesses, this _____ day of_____, 20_____.

Signed:_____

_____
Official Capacity of Officer

First Codicil to the Will of

_____

I, _____, a resident of _____ County, _____ declare this to be the first codicil to my Last Will and Testament dated _____, _____.

FIRST: I hereby revoke the clause of my Will which reads as follows:
_____
_____
_____
_____.

SECOND: I hereby add the following clause to my Will: _____
_____
_____
_____
_____.

THIRD: In all other respects I hereby confirm and republish my Last Will and Testament dated _____, _____.

IN WITNESS WHEREOF, I have signed, published, and declared the foregoing instrument as and for a codicil to my Last Will and Testament, this _____ day of _____, 20_____.

_____

The foregoing instrument was on the _____day of _____, _____, signed at the end thereof, and at the same time published and declared by _____, as and for a codicil to his/her Last Will and Testament, dated _____, 20_____, in the presence of each of us, who, this attestation clause having been read to us, did at the request of the said testator/testatrix, in his/her presence and in the presence of each other signed our names as witnesses thereto.

_____residing at_____

_____residing at_____

_____residing at_____

Self-Proved Codicil Affidavit

(attach to Codicil)

STATE OF _____

COUNTY OF _____

    We, _____ and _____ and _____, the testator and the witnesses, whose names are signed to the attached or foregoing instrument in those capacities, personally appearing before the undersigned authority and being first duly sworn, declare to the undersigned authority under penalty of perjury that: 1) the testator declared, signed, and executed the instrument as a codicil to his or her last will; 2) he or she signed it willingly, or directed another to sign for him or her; 3) he or she executed it as his or her free and voluntary act for the purposes therein expressed; and 4) each of the witnesses, and the request of the testator, in his or her hearing and presence and in the presence of each other, signed the will as witnesses, and that to the best of his or her knowledge the testator was at that time of full legal age, of sound mind, and under no constraint or undue influence.

_____ (Testator)

_____ (Witness)

_____ (Witness)

Subscribed, sworn, and acknowledged before me _____ a notary public, and by _____, the testator, and by _____ and _____, witnesses, this _____ day of _____, 20____.

_____

Notary public

Self-Proved Codicil Affidavit
(attach to Will)

STATE OF _____

COUNTY OF _____

    I, the undersigned, an officer authorized to administer oaths, certify that _____, the testator and _____ and _____, the witnesses, whose names are signed to the attached or foregoing instrument and whose signatures appear below, having appeared before me and having first been duly sworn, each then declared to me that: 1) the attached or foregoing instrument is a codicil to the last will of the testator; 2) the testator willingly and voluntarily declared, signed, and executed the will in the presence of the witnesses; 3) the witnesses signed the will upon the request of the testator, in the presence and hearing of the testator and in the presence of each other; 4) to the best knowledge of each witness, the testator was, at the time of signing, of the age of majority (or otherwise legally competent to make a will), of sound mind and memory, and under no constraint or undue influence; and 5) each witness was and is competent and of proper age to witness a codicil to a will.

_____ (Testator)

_____ (Witness)

_____ (Witness)

Subscribed and sworn to before me by _____, the testator, who is personally known to me or who has produced _____ as identification, and by _____ a witness who is personally known to me or who has produced _____ as identification, and by _____, a witness, who is personally known to me or who has produced _____ as identification, this _____ day of_____, 20____.

_____
Notary or other officer

Self-Proved Codicil Affidavit
(attach to Codicil)

STATE OF TEXAS

COUNTY OF _____

    Before me, the undersigned authority, on this day personally appeared _____ _____, _____, and _____ _____, known to me to be the testator and the witnesses, respectively, whose names are subscribed to the annexed or foregoing instrument in their respective capacities, and, all of said persons being by me duly sworn, the said _____ _____ testator, declared to me and to the said witnesses in my presence that said instrument is his or her codicil, and that he or she had willingly made and executed it as his or her free act and deed, and the said witnesses, each on his or her oath stated to me in the presence and hearing of the said testator, that the said testator had declared to them that said instrument is his or her codicil, and that he or she executed same as such and wanted each of them to sign it as a witness; and upon their oaths each witness stated further that they did sign the same as witnesses in the presence of the said testator and at his or her request; that he or she was at the time eighteen years of age or over (or being under such age, was or had been lawfully married, or was then a member of the armed forces of the United States or an auxiliary thereof or of the Maritime Service) and was of sound mind; and that each of said witnesses was then at least fourteen years of age.

_____ (Testator)

_____ (Witness)

_____ (Witness)

Subscribed and sworn to before me by _____, the testator, and by _____, _____, and _____, the witnesses, this _____ day of_____, 20____.

Signed:_____

_____
Official Capacity of Officer

LIVING WILL

I, _____, being of sound mind willfully and voluntarily make known my desires regarding my medical care and treatment under the circumstances as indicated below:

_____ 1. If I should have an incurable or irreversible condition that will cause my death within a relatively short time, and if I am unable to make decisions regarding my medical treatment, I direct my attending physician to withhold or withdraw procedures that merely prolong the dying process and are not necessary to my comfort or to alleviate pain. This authorization includes, but is not limited to, the withholding or the withdrawal of the following types of medical treatment (subject to any special instructions in paragraph 5 below):

    _____ a. Artificial feeding and hydration.
    _____ b. Cardiopulmonary resuscitation (this includes, but is not limited to, the use of drugs, electric shock, and artificial breathing).
    _____ c. Kidney dialysis.
    _____ d. Surgery or other invasive procedures.
    _____ e. Drugs and antibiotics.
    _____ f. Transfusions of blood or blood products.
    _____ g. Other: _____
                           _____

_____ 2. If I should be in an irreversible coma or persistent vegetative state that my attending physician reasonably believes to be irreversible or incurable, I direct my attending physician to withhold or withdraw medical procedures and treatment other than such medical procedures and treatment necessary to my comfort or to alleviate pain. This authorization includes, but is not limited to, the withholding or withdrawal of the following types of medical treatment (subject to any special instructions in paragraph 5 below):

    _____ a. Artificial feeding and hydration.
    _____ b. Cardiopulmonary resuscitation (this includes, but is not limited to, the use of drugs, electric shock, and artificial breathing).
    _____ c. Kidney dialysis.
    _____ d. Surgery or other invasive procedures.
    _____ e. Drugs and antibiotics.
    _____ f. Transfusions of blood or blood products.
    _____ g. Other: _____
                           _____

_____ 3. If I have a medical condition where I am unable to communicate my desires as to treatment and my physician determines that the burdens of treatment outweigh the expected benefits, I direct my attending physician to withhold or withdraw medical procedures and treatment other than such medical procedures and treatment necessary to my comfort or to alleviate pain. This authorization includes, but is not limited to, the withholding or withdrawal of the following types of medical treatment (subject to any special instructions in paragraph 5 below):

    _____ a. Artificial feeding and hydration.
    _____ b. Cardiopulmonary resuscitation (this includes, but is not limited to, the use of drugs, electric shock, and artificial breathing).
    _____ c. Kidney dialysis.
    _____ d. Surgery or other invasive procedures.
    _____ e. Drugs and antibiotics.
    _____ f. Transfusions of blood or blood products.

129

_____ g. Other: _____
_____

_____ 4. I want my life prolonged to the greatest extent possible (subject to any special instructions in paragraph 5 below).

_____ 5. Special instructions (if any) _____
_____
_____
_____

Signed this _____ day of _____,200____.

Signature _____

Address:_____

_____

The declarant is personally known to me and voluntarily signed this document in my presence.

Witness:_____   Witness_____

Name:_____   Name:_____

Address:_____   Address:_____

_____   _____

State of _____)
County of _____)

On this _____ day of _____, 200_____, before me, personally appeared
_____, principal, and
_____ and _____,
witnesses, who are personally known to me or who provided _____
_____
as identification, and signed the foregoing instrument in my presence.

_____
Notary Public

UNIFORM DONOR CARD

The undersigned hereby makes this anatomical gift, if medically acceptable, to take effect on death. The words and marks below indicate my desires:

I give:

      (a) ____ any needed organs or parts;

      (b) ____ only the following organs or parts

_____

for the purpose of transplantation, therapy, medical research, or education;

      (c) ____ my body for anatomical study if needed.

Limitations or special wishes, if any:

_____

Signed by the donor and the following witnesses in the presence of each other:

_____	_____
Signature of Donor	Date of birth
_____	_____
Date signed	City & State
_____	_____
Witness	Witness
_____	_____
Address	Address

UNIFORM DONOR CARD

The undersigned hereby makes this anatomical gift, if medically acceptable, to take effect on death. The words and marks below indicate my desires:

I give:

      (a) ____ any needed organs or parts;

      (b) ____ only the following organs or parts

_____

for the purpose of transplantation, therapy, medical research, or education;

      (c) ____ my body for anatomical study if needed.

Limitations or special wishes, if any:

_____

Signed by the donor and the following witnesses in the presence of each other:

_____	_____
Signature of Donor	Date of birth
_____	_____
Date signed	City & State
_____	_____
Witness	Witness
_____	_____
Address	Address

UNIFORM DONOR CARD

The undersigned hereby makes this anatomical gift, if medically acceptable, to take effect on death. The words and marks below indicate my desires:

I give:

      (a) ____ any needed organs or parts;

      (b) ____ only the following organs or parts

_____

for the purpose of transplantation, therapy, medical research, or education;

      (c) ____ my body for anatomical study if needed.

Limitations or special wishes, if any:

_____

Signed by the donor and the following witnesses in the presence of each other:

_____	_____
Signature of Donor	Date of birth
_____	_____
Date signed	City & State
_____	_____
Witness	Witness
_____	_____
Address	Address

UNIFORM DONOR CARD

The undersigned hereby makes this anatomical gift, if medically acceptable, to take effect on death. The words and marks below indicate my desires:

I give:

      (a) ____ any needed organs or parts;

      (b) ____ only the following organs or parts

_____

for the purpose of transplantation, therapy, medical research, or education;

      (c) ____ my body for anatomical study if needed.

Limitations or special wishes, if any:

_____

Signed by the donor and the following witnesses in the presence of each other:

_____	_____
Signature of Donor	Date of birth
_____	_____
Date signed	City & State
_____	_____
Witness	Witness
_____	_____
Address	Address

One of these cards should be cut out and carried in your wallet or purse.

131

INDEX

Your #1 Source for Real World Legal Information...

SPHINX® PUBLISHING
A Division of Sourcebooks, Inc.®

- Written by lawyers
- Simple English explanation of the law
- Forms and instructions included

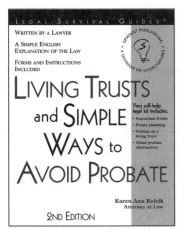

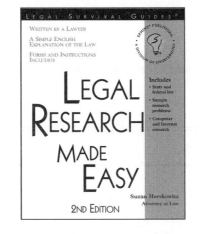

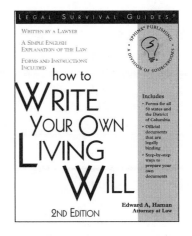

LIVING TRUSTS AND SIMPLE WAYS TO AVOID PROBATE, 2ND ED.

Explains how probate works and what a living trust can do that a will cannot. Illustrates simple ways to avoid probate and save hundreds of dollars.

176 pages; $22.95;
ISBN 1-57071-336-7

LEGAL RESEARCH MADE EASY, 2ND ED.

Simplify the process of doing your own legal research in law libraries and on computers. This book explains how to research statutes, case law, databases, law reports, and more. Learn how to access your state's statutes on the Internet. Save enormous amounts of time and money by handling your own legal research.

128 pages; $19.95;
ISBN 1-57071-400-2

HOW TO WRITE YOUR OWN LIVING WILL, 2ND ED.

Without a living will, doctors and hospitals may give you medical treatment you would not want at a time when you are unable to make your own choices known. A living will allows a person to make the choice, while well, of what medical procedures should be used in case of terminal illness.

176 pages; $16.95;
ISBN 1-57248-118-8

See the following order form for books written specifically for California, Florida, Georgia, Illinois, Massachusetts, Michigan, Minnesota, New York, North Carolina, Ohio, Pennsylvania, and Texas!

What our customers say about our books:

"It couldn't be more clear for the lay person." —R.D.

"I want you to know I really appreciate your book. It has saved me a lot of time and money." —L.T.

"Your real estate contracts book has saved me nearly $12,000.00 in closing costs over the past year." —A.B.

"...many of the legal questions that I have had over the years were answered clearly and concisely through your plain English interpretation of the law." —C.E.H.

"If there weren't people out there like you I'd be lost. You have the best books of this type out there." —S.B.

"...your forms and directions are easy to follow." —C.V.M.

Sphinx Publishing's Legal Survival Guides
are directly available from the Sourcebooks, Inc., or from your local bookstores.
For credit card orders call 1–800–43–BRIGHT, write P.O. Box 4410, Naperville, IL 60567-4410,
or fax 630-961-2168

SPHINX® PUBLISHING'S NATIONAL TITLES

Valid in All 50 States

LEGAL SURVIVAL IN BUSINESS

How to Form a Limited Liability Company	$19.95
How to Form Your Own Corporation (3E)	$19.95
How to Form Your Own Partnership	$19.95
How to Register Your Own Copyright (3E)	$19.95
How to Register Your Own Trademark (3E)	$19.95
Most Valuable Business Legal Forms You'll Ever Need (2E)	$19.95
Most Valuable Corporate Forms You'll Ever Need (2E)	$24.95
Software Law (with diskette)	$29.95

LEGAL SURVIVAL IN COURT

Crime Victim's Guide to Justice	$19.95
Debtors' Rights (3E)	$12.95
Grandparents' Rights (2E)	$19.95
Help Your Lawyer Win Your Case (2E)	$12.95
Jurors' Rights (2E)	$9.95
Legal Research Made Easy (2E)	$14.95
Winning Your Personal Injury Claim	$19.95

LEGAL SURVIVAL IN REAL ESTATE

How to Buy a Condominium or Townhome	$16.95
How to Negotiate Real Estate Contracts (3E)	$16.95
How to Negotiate Real Estate Leases (3E)	$16.95

LEGAL SURVIVAL IN PERSONAL AFFAIRS

Guia de Inmigracion a Estados Unidos (2E)	$19.95
How to File Your Own Bankruptcy (4E)	$19.95
How to File Your Own Divorce (4E)	$19.95
How to Make Your Own Will (2E)	$12.95
How to Write Your Own Living Will (2E)	$12.95
How to Write Your Own Premarital Agreement (2E)	$19.95
How to Win Your Unemployment Compensation Claim	$19.95
Living Trusts and Simple Ways to Avoid Probate (2E)	$19.95
Most Valuable Personal Legal Forms You Will Ever Need	$19.95
Neighbor v. Neighbor (2E)	$12.95
The Nanny and Domestic Help Legal Kit	$19.95
The Power of Attorney Handbook (3E)	$19.95
Quick Divorce Book	$19.95
Social Security Benefits Handbook (2E)	$14.95
Unmarried Parents' Rights	$19.95
U.S.A. Immigration Guide (3E)	$19.95
Your Right to Child Custody, Visitation and Support	$19.95

Legal Survival Guides are directly available from Sourcebooks, Inc., or from your local bookstores.
Prices are subject to change without notice.

For credit card orders call 1–800–43–BRIGHT, write P.O. Box 4410, Naperville, IL 60567-4410
or fax 630-961-2168

SPHINX® PUBLISHING ORDER FORM

BILL TO:		SHIP TO:		
Phone #	Terms	F.O.B.	Chicago, IL	Ship Date

Charge my: ☐ VISA ☐ MasterCard ☐ American Express

☐ **Money Order or Personal Check**

Credit Card Number

Expiration Date

Qty	ISBN	Title	Retail	Ext.
		SPHINX PUBLISHING NATIONAL TITLES		
___	1-57071-166-6	Crime Victim's Guide to Justice	$19.95	___
___	1-57071-342-1	Debtors' Rights (3E)	$12.95	___
___	1-57248-082-3	Grandparents' Rights (2E)	$19.95	___
___	1-57248-087-4	Guia de Inmigracion a Estados Unidos (2E)	$19.95	___
___	1-57248-103-X	Help Your Lawyer Win Your Case (2E)	$12.95	___
___	1-57071-164-X	How to Buy a Condominium or Townhome	$16.95	___
___	1-57071-223-9	How to File Your Own Bankruptcy (4E)	$19.95	___
___	1-57248-132-3	How to File Your Own Divorce (4E)	$19.95	___
___	1-57248-100-5	How to Form a DE Corporation from Any State	$19.95	___
___	1-57248-083-1	How to Form a Limited Liability Company	$19.95	___
___	1-57248-101-3	How to Form a NV Corporation from Any State	$19.95	___
___	1-57248-099-8	How to Form a Nonprofit Corporation	$24.95	___
___	1-57248-133-1	How to Form Your Own Corporation (3E)	$19.95	___
___	1-57071-343-X	How to Form Your Own Partnership	$19.95	___
___	1-57248-119-6	How to Make Your Own Will (2E)	$12.95	___
___	1-57071-331-6	How to Negotiate Real Estate Contracts (3E)	$16.95	___
___	1-57071-332-4	How to Negotiate Real Estate Leases (3E)	$16.95	___
___	1-57248-124-2	How to Register Your Own Copyright (3E)	$19.95	___
___	1-57248-104-8	How to Register Your Own Trademark (3E)	$19.95	___
___	1-57071-349-9	How to Win Your Unemployment Compensation Claim	$19.95	___
___	1-57248-118-8	How to Write Your Own Living Will (2E)	$12.95	___
___	1-57071-344-8	How to Write Your Own Premarital Agreement (2E)	$19.95	___
___	1-57071-333-2	Jurors' Rights (2E)	$9.95	___
___	1-57071-400-2	Legal Research Made Easy (2E)	$14.95	___
___	1-57071-336-7	Living Trusts and Simple Ways to Avoid Probate (2E)	$19.95	___
___	1-57071-345-6	Most Valuable Bus. Legal Forms You'll Ever Need (2E)	$19.95	___
___	1-57071-346-4	Most Valuable Corporate Forms You'll Ever Need (2E)	$24.95	___
___	1-57248-130-7	Most Valuable Personal Legal Forms You'll Ever Need	$19.95	___
___	1-57248-098-X	The Nanny and Domestic Help Legal Kit	$19.95	___
___	1-57248-089-0	Neighbor v. Neighbor (2E)	$14.95	___
___	1-57071-348-0	The Power of Attorney Handbook (3E)	$19.95	___
___	1-57248-131-5	Quick Divorce Boook	$19.95	___
___	1-57071-337-5	Social Security Benefits Handbook (2E)	$14.95	___
___	1-57071-163-1	Software Law (w/diskette)	$29.95	___
___	1-57071-399-5	Unmarried Parents' Rights	$19.95	___
___	1-57071-354-5	U.S.A. Immigration Guide (3E)	$19.95	___
___	1-57071-165-8	Winning Your Personal Injury Claim	$19.95	___
___	1-57248-097-1	Your Right to Child Custody, Visitation and Support	$19.95	___
		CALIFORNIA TITLES		
___	1-57071-360-X	CA Power of Attorney Handbook	$12.95	___
___	1-57248-126-9	How to File for Divorce in CA (2E)	$19.95	___
___	1-57071-356-1	How to Make a CA Will	$12.95	___
___	1-57071-358-8	How to Win in Small Claims Court in CA	$14.95	___
___	1-57071-359-6	Landlords' Rights and Duties in CA	$19.95	___
		FLORIDA TITLES		
___	1-57071-363-4	Florida Power of Attorney Handbook (2E)	$12.95	___
___	1-57248-093-9	How to File for Divorce in FL (6E)	$24.95	___
___	1-57071-380-4	How to Form a Corporation in FL (4E)	$19.95	___
___	1-57248-086-6	How to Form a Limited Liability Co. in FL	$19.95	___
___	1-57071-401-0	How to Form a Partnership in FL	$19.95	___
___	1-57248-113-7	How to Make a FL Will (6E)	$12.95	___
___	1-57248-088-2	How to Modify Your FL Divorce Judgment (4E)	$22.95	___
___		***Form Continued on Following Page***	**SUBTOTAL**	___

To order, call Sourcebooks at 1-800-43-BRIGHT or FAX (630)961-2168 (Bookstores, libraries, wholesalers—please call for discount)

Prices are subject to change without notice.

SPHINX® PUBLISHING ORDER FORM

Qty	ISBN	Title	Retail	Ext.
_____	1-57248-081-5	How to Start a Business in FL (5E)	$16.95	_____
_____	1-57071-362-6	How to Win in Small Claims Court in FL (6E)	$14.95	_____
_____	1-57248-123-4	Landlords' Rights and Duties in FL (8E)	$19.95	_____
		GEORGIA TITLES		
_____	1-57071-376-6	How to File for Divorce in GA (3E)	$19.95	_____
_____	1-57248-075-0	How to Make a GA Will (3E)	$12.95	_____
_____	1-57248-076-9	How to Start a Business in Georgia	$16.95	_____
		ILLINOIS TITLES		
_____	1-57071-405-3	How to File for Divorce in IL (2E)	$19.95	_____
_____	1-57071-415-0	How to Make an IL Will (2E)	$12.95	_____
_____	1-57071-416-9	How to Start a Business in IL (2E)	$16.95	_____
_____	1-57248-078-5	Landlords' Rights & Duties in IL	$19.95	_____
		MASSACHUSETTS TITLES		
_____	1-57071-329-4	How to File for Divorce in MA (2E)	$19.95	_____
_____	1-57248-115-3	How to Form a Corporation in MA	$19.95	_____
_____	1-57248-108-0	How to Make a MA Will (2E)	$12.95	_____
_____	1-57248-106-4	How to Start a Business in MA (2E)	$16.95	_____
_____	1-57248-107-2	Landlords' Rights and Duties in MA (2E)	$19.95	_____
		MICHIGAN TITLES		
_____	1-57071-409-6	How to File for Divorce in MI (2E)	$19.95	_____
_____	1-57248-077-7	How to Make a MI Will (2E)	$12.95	_____
_____	1-57071-407-X	How to Start a Business in MI (2E)	$16.95	_____
		NEW YORK TITLES		
_____	1-57071-184-4	How to File for Divorce in NY	$24.95	_____
_____	1-57248-105-6	How to Form a Corporation in NY	$19.95	_____
_____	1-57248-095-5	How to Make a NY Will (2E)	$12.95	_____
_____	1-57071-185-2	How to Start a Business in NY	$16.95	_____
_____	1-57071-187-9	How to Win in Small Claims Court in NY	$14.95	_____
_____	1-57071-186-0	Landlords' Rights and Duties in NY	$19.95	_____

Qty	ISBN	Title	Retail	Ext.
_____	1-57071-188-7	New York Power of Attorney Handbook	$19.95	_____
_____	1-57248-122-6	Tenants' Rights in NY	$19..95	_____
		NORTH CAROLINA TITLES		
_____	1-57071-326-X	How to File for Divorce in NC (2E)	$19.95	_____
_____	1-57248-129-3	How to Make a NC Will (3E)	$12.95	_____
_____	1-57248-096-3	How to Start a Business in NC (2E)	$16.95	_____
_____	1-57248-091-2	Landlords' Rights & Duties in NC	$19.95	_____
		OHIO TITLES		
_____	1-57248-102-1	How to File for Divorce in OH	$19.95	_____
		PENNSYLVANIA TITLES		
_____	1-57248-127-7	How to File for Divorce in PA (2E)	$19.95	_____
_____	1-57248-094-7	How to Make a PA Will (2E)	$12.95	_____
_____	1-57248-112-9	How to Start a Business in PA (2E)	$16.95	_____
_____	1-57071-179-8	Landlords' Rights and Duties in PA	$19.95	_____
		TEXAS TITLES		
_____	1-57071-330-8	How to File for Divorce in TX (2E)	$19.95	_____
_____	1-57248-114-5	How to Form a Corporation in TX (2E)	$19.95	_____
_____	1-57071-417-7	How to Make a TX Will (2E)	$12.95	_____
_____	1-57071-418-5	How to Probate an Estate in TX (2E)	$19.95	_____
_____	1-57071-365-0	How to Start a Business in TX (2E)	$16.95	_____
_____	1-57248-111-0	How to Win in Small Claims Court in TX (2E)	$14.95	_____
_____	1-57248-110-2	Landlords' Rights and Duties in TX (2E)	$19.95	_____

SUBTOTAL THIS PAGE _____

SUBTOTAL PREVIOUS PAGE _____

Illinois residents add 6.75% sales tax _____

Florida residents add 6% state sales tax plus applicable discretionary surtax _____

Shipping— $4.00 for 1st book, $1.00 each additional _____

TOTAL _____

To order, call Sourcebooks at 1-800-43-BRIGHT or FAX (630)961-2168 (Bookstores, libraries, wholesalers—please call for discount)

Prices are subject to change without notice.